MW00897896

With Love
Aline Umutoni

FROM BONDAGE TO FREEDOM

How God Turned My Pain into a Purpose
and My Mess into a Message

Aline Umutoni

WESTBOW
PRESS®
A DIVISION OF THOMAS NELSON
& ZONDERVAN

WestBow Press books may be ordered through booksellers or by contacting:

WestBow Press
A Division of Thomas Nelson & Zondervan
1663 Liberty Drive
Bloomington, IN 47403
www.westbowpress.com
1 (866) 928-1240

ISBN: 978-1-9736-8168-7 (sc)
ISBN: 978-1-9736-8170-0 (hc)
ISBN: 978-1-9736-8169-4 (e)

Print information available on the last page.

WestBow Press rev. date: 12/05/2019

This book was written for all the people who once felt they had nothing to give and felt unworthy because they went through painful situations that shut down their dreams. It is for all the women who were told that they could never achieve their dreams because of their painful past. This book will bring light to all who were broken and are still in need of healing. This light will restore all that the enemy has stolen from the lives of the readers.

Acknowledgments

I cannot thank God enough for trusting me to write this book for His people. I am grateful for the opportunity to share my story with the world and to let God impact one life at a time as I lay down my life to serve the one and only Savior, Jesus Christ.

I would like to thank all the people God put in my life who encouraged me through my pain and the healing process. I cannot name every person who supported me, but I would like to name a few who, by their obedience to God, made this dream come true. I would like to thank my family in South Africa, Rwanda, Norway, and France for helping me with my healing process and for encouraging me to write this book when I thought I could not do it on my own. I also thank my spiritual parents who risked their lives to protect me when I left the house of oppression. To my late Aunt Umulisa and my late Uncle Claude, who went to heaven before this book was published. I love you and miss you so much. Lastly, I would like to thank my friends and family in Christ who prayed for me and walked with me through the process. I thank Nida and Rico Almodiel, Kemi Duro-Emmanuel, Ingrid Sidibe, Danielle Vario and Diane Gibbs. I love you all so much and pray that God blesses you mightily.

Contents

Introduction

My name is Aline Umutoni. I was born in Rwanda and raised in many countries. My story is one of learning to trust, and of overcoming through the grace of God.

From an early age, I learned to survive and fight battles that were brought through horrific events in my life. I lost my mother who died in a car accident when I was thirteen months old, and then my father who was killed in the Rwandan genocide against Tutsis of 1994 when I was five years old.

Left with no parents, I turned my love and attention to my grandmother, who always showed me love and care. She passed away a few years after the genocide. After her death, I went from being loved to being sexually abused, and went from being an innocent child to a being a broken teenager. I lost hope in life and contemplated suicide. But, my hopelessness never stopped God from sending help through people who always reminded me of God's love for me. God still loved me in spite of all the hurt and brokenness I faced at a young age. Even at times when I lost my faith in God, He used people to remind me of how blessed I was in Him. This helped me believe that all the pain I was facing was not intended to destroy me, but that one day I would look back and see a purpose in every step of my life. I started to believe that I was not suffering because of my pain alone, but for those who would one day see God in every step of their lives as they would hear my testimony and about my walk with Him.

After my first encounter with Jesus, I decided to fight for my freedom with everything I had. Three years later, when the day finally arrived, I took my first step to freedom. I finally learned to live in a place where no one was there to hurt me. I took my first breath of freedom after thirteen years of bondage.

I wrote this book as a testimony of God's faithfulness and triumph, and will share the events that shaped my life and led to my freedom. For the sake of privacy, I will not mention the names of people to preserve their identities in the book. This book was not written to be a succession of events that portray atrocities done to me, but to share the goodness and love of our Lord Jesus Christ and His faithfulness through it all.

Although life may sometimes overtake us, we should always be reminded that Jesus overcame the world. I pray that as you read this book you have healing and hope in God to deliver you from any situation you have faced in the past, face in the present, or will face in the future. I pray that this book will give you endurance and perseverance in God to know that nothing is impossible with Him. I pray that all the dreams that were killed or destroyed through abuse and past hurts will come to life and bring a greater purpose for everyone who faces their pain. I pray that you will embrace who you are and what you went through so that God can heal you, and most importantly, impact other people as you walk in wholeness seeing yourself as an answer to someone else's pain.

I believe that I faced all the pain and trouble in my life so that today I may be healed and write this book to bring healing to other women like me who were once hurt and lost all hope for the future. God has something greater for you than your pain. You can only see God's plan, when you allow Him to heal you. God will then reveal the purpose behind the pain and hardships you had to face. God has great plans for your life.

I pray that all abused women, men, orphans, and rejected persons who read this book will get a revelation about why God allowed all the hurt they faced and will give them the purpose behind the pain. I hope my testimony brings healing to anyone who reads this book. I believe that my story will encourage an orphan to know they are not alone, a rejected person to rise above the rejection and know that they are loved, and an abused woman to know that she matters.

Whatever situation you are facing, you should never stop believing that there is a brighter future in front of you. God's mercy and power is available for you to find joy and healing in all areas of your life. Always know that God is with you. Although we may not have similar pain, I believe that God will heal your pain and you will find meaning in your trials. He will set you free from every chain and will heal you as you read this book.

May the Lord bless you and encounter you in every line of the book. To God be the glory and power forever and ever. Amen.

In God's love,
Aline Umutoni

CHAPTER 1
Hidden Truth

I fought God's direction for me to write this book. It took me five years to realize that I could not do it on my own. I was afraid to share my story with people because of the fear of rejection. I was afraid that people would see me differently after they read what happened to me: how I survived genocide and how I was mistreated and abused in my teenage years. I felt that my story was too painful to share. I never liked being a victim and certainly did not want my story to portray me as one. I thought exposing my scars would bring more pain to me, so I chose to keep my story to myself, my close friends, and my family.

Throughout five years of denying my purpose, God still blessed and sustained me in all my works even though it was not His plan for me while I was walking a path that He had not created me to walk on. I was a people pleaser and needed to be validated by others. I wanted to be acknowledged, and I worked hard to be the best in all my endeavors so that I could have the praise of people instead of God.

The more I ran toward my personal goals, the emptier I felt. I always wanted to show the people who hurt me how I could succeed without their help in my life. I was grateful that God delivered me from the house of oppression (where my innocence was taken) as He promised, and I was determined to work hard so I could be independent and do the work of God on my own terms. I wanted to serve God with my life, but I was not ready to surrender my life fully and give Him my career and my dreams. I was praying and serving God in my work, but I did not realize that God had more in store for me. I was reaching out of my comfort zone by giving to His church and to people in need, but I had not given my heart fully to God.

I always told myself that I went to church, tithed, and shared the good news of the Gospel wherever I went, I was doing what God wanted from me, but I was wrong! I was pursuing my own dreams. I would share the good news and pray for people around me without sharing my story because I thought it was only for me and my family to know about. "The secrets must remain hidden" was the lie the enemy made me believe.

I knew God and loved Him with all my heart because He had shown me His face and His goodness when He delivered me from the house of oppression. I knew God had saved me for a reason, and I was determined to never forget Him in all my works. I knew His presence was with me, and I vowed to follow Him all the days of my life.

I never prayed to God to ask Him my purpose because I was convinced that His purpose for me was in my dreams and my personal goals. I was focused on myself and fulfilling my dreams. It was only in 2016 that I began to ask God if my dreams were His plan for my life. A part of me did not ask God about His dream for my life because I did not want to hear anything in opposition to my ideas.

My dream job was to be a hydrogeologist. Hydrogeology studies the occurrence, distribution, and effect of groundwater and the geological aspects of surface water. My goal was to provide clean water to remote places in Africa where people must walk many miles to get clean water for their families.

I had this dream since I was a teenager. When I was sixteen years old, I started having dreams of rivers and streams flowing with treasures underneath. It made me a lover of nature and water from a young age. To me, nature was a representation of the glorious power of our God. When I was finally given the chance to pursue my dreams, I gave my all because I believed my dreams were God's. I was given a chance to study geology and hydrogeology eventually when I was out of the abuse. My passion for water and rocks was the best opportunity to pursue what I had always dreamed about. My vision was to help people who could not help themselves by pursuing a career that makes a difference in communities; however, I did not realize that God's plans for me were not as obvious as I thought. Jesus says in John 4:13-14, that He is the living water, and whoever drinks of Him will never thirst again. I did not realize that as I drank of His living water, and as I experienced His power, Jesus wanted me to share His goodness with the world just as the Samaritan woman did in John 4:39. The Samaritan woman did not keep to herself what happened to her at the well. She chose to share her testimony with the entire town and with the people she was hiding from when she came to the well at noon. She shared the good news with the people who would mock her because of her lifestyle. The Bible says that she went to the well at noon so she would not be disturbed (John 4:6). Her life was not the best example in her community, and she was not a normal woman like other Samaritan women. She had had five husbands and was with another man when she encountered Jesus (John 4:17-18).

When I studied this story in John 4, I identified with the Samaritan woman. I had not had five husbands, but I did have an unusual past that made me different from other women in my community and in my family. I did not look like the people around me wherever I would go. I had many scars that I tried to hide from people. I always thought my scars and my story were not worthy of sharing. I tried to hide it as much as I could, and I would choose to share some parts of it, but not the full story, because I was afraid of being rejected. I tried to fit in by hiding what I had gone through so I could be loved and accepted.

Then, in 2016, after a few years of running away from my ultimate purpose and not listening to God about writing this book, He opened a door for me to go to the United States to pursue my studies, as He had promised. I was excited to see that all my dreams were coming to pass, and I was grateful that He gave me the opportunity to do what I loved.

I did not know that my trip to the United States was not to fulfill my dreams, but to discover my purpose and to surrender to God completely. One evening, as I was praying for direction, the Holy Spirit asked me to give Him all of me and all my crowns (everything I held dear: my career, my job, my family, etc.). That was one of the most painful things I've ever had to do because I loved and I was devoted to all the things God asked me to give to Him.

When I got to the United States, I felt like I was at the peak of my life. I was pursuing my dreams walking in the path I had always prayed for and things seemed to work according to my plans, but I did not have the peace and the joy of the Lord in my heart.

On the outside, everything looked well, but I was at the end of myself, was tired of running after futile things that could not fulfill my heart, was not affecting people around me, and was focused on what I could get to promote myself. I was tired of trying to fit in and wearing a mask to hide my scars, not being true to myself and who I was in Christ.

I had a painful decision to make that would require me to let go of everything I knew and reach toward the unknown. I prayed asking God to have His way in me and surrendered everything that I thought defined me. This decision was not easy, but was scary and unpredictable to me because I had always planned every aspect of my life.

I chose to surrender and follow God's calling and purpose for my life, which required me to let go of many things that I had built and held dear in my pursuit of what I believed success was, to focus on what God created me to accomplish on the earth after the realization that His plans were greater than mine. So, I put my life and future in God's hands, not knowing what would be next. Geology had been my joy and fulfillment on the outside, but not from within. I then turned to God to find my joy and fulfillment in Him. Laying down my whole life at the altar of grace was the most difficult decision I have ever made, but the level of fulfillment I had afterward was priceless. The peace of God in my life was beyond reach and understanding. I was walking on the waters of faith, but had more joy and peace than I ever had when pursuing my dreams.

After repositioning myself to what God had created me to accomplish, in November 2017 God gave me a word that it was time for me to write this book. I was no longer afraid to share my entire story and had been healed of the scars that I had in my heart. God redeemed me and gave me the healing to share my story, so that many may find hope and healing as I did.

God used one of the friends I was fortunate to meet, and she provided all the tools I needed to write this book. I believe she was the hands and feet of Jesus in my life, and she pushed me to start writing a few weeks after I met her. I started to write my first chapter on December 2, 2017 and could not stop writing until it was finished. The Spirit of God gave me the words to write and gave me the revelation behind this book. While writing every chapter, God was healing some part of my heart that still needed healing.

As I wrote every word, I felt the breath of the Holy Spirit flow into the lines. That's where I had a deeper revelation of the true author and owner of this book: it belongs to God, and I am just a vessel used to write all that He desires for His children to know so that they can find healing from their pain and see the purpose behind it. The Spirit of God gave me the words to write every chapter so that God may be glorified and His name may be lifted in the lives of all who read it. I believe this book is carrying His presence and His living water that will fill your heart and satisfy your thirst forever.

I finally understood why it took me five years before I could write this book. It was because I had to heal from the inside out and lay down my life so that God could use me to write it. I had to die to myself so that I could focus on what God would do through me and not on what He could do for me as Paul stated in Galatians 2:20. Moreover, since I had very low self-esteem, I had to learn to see myself the way God sees me and heal me from all the words that were said to me when I was growing up. Until I was fully healed, I could not see my story and my pain as a purpose to show God's faithfulness and bring hope to others. Because I was ashamed of my roots and my past, I was defined by it and had not found the peace to take up my cross and follow Christ. I compared myself to others and always felt damaged and irreparable as my standards were described by the world and not by God. Because of my need for validation and acceptance, I did not go against my family's decision to keep my story private. I was compelled to keep it for myself, so I could please many and be on everyone's side.

My perception as a survivor was not as a conqueror, but as a victim. I thought I was ready to move on with my life without sharing my story, but the enemy would always remind me of my past and show me how I could not run away from it. When I surrendered all of myself to God, I realized that I was not saved to survive, but to thrive and bring healing and hope to others by sharing what God has done in my life and where He took me from, so that many may see His faithfulness through my walk with Him.

I doubted that God could use my story to inspire other women until I was given an opportunity to share my story multiple times a few months before I started to write the book. That is when I started to see the impact it had on women I never knew, which gave me the peace to write this book. I believe that God will use this book to heal women I will never be fortunate enough to meet in person this side of heaven.

This book is not just telling a story, but is the testimony of a woman who thought she had nothing to give to the body of Christ, was not good at writing, and had English as her second language. God has gracefully given me the ability to write this book in a language that I am not very confident in, to show anyone who reads this book that God can do wonders by using the foolish things of the world to confound the wise as it says in 1 Corinthians 1:27.

I would like to encourage you to know that God will qualify you for where He wants to take you, and He will equip you with all that you need to fulfill His will. However, you cannot get it done if you are not willing to walk by faith and not by sight. God can take the worst part of your story and turn it into beauty for His glory; He can turn your ashes into beauty (Isaiah 61:3).

I saw God not only healing me, but restoring my brokenness and using my pain as a platform to heal many and bring them to Him. I encourage you to lean into His presence and let Him heal you from all that you have gone through. Pour your heart into Him and let Him heal you and use your pain and experience to save many because we overcome by the blood of the Lamb and the word of our testimony (Revelation 12:11). I came to understand that no testimony or story is too bad or too ugly for God to use for His glory. God can take us through the fire so that we can grow stronger in Him and be His advocate wherever He takes us.

Jesus came to earth so we might have life and life more abundantly. Since we are His hands and feet, God restores us so we can share His goodness with those around us. We are called to show the light of Christ by what God entrusted us to carry. Our story is one of the things God entrusted us with because He always gives us what we have the capacity to carry. When we overcome our trials and walk victoriously with God, He wants us to share and give hope to many others who may be going through similar situations to what you have overcome.

When God asked me to write this book, I thought it would be written in French and later translated in English, because I am more comfortable writing in French than in English. He wanted me to rely on Him for every word I would write because I have never felt comfortable writing in English. In fact, all of my prayers and journaling are done in French. Hence, writing the book in English required me to rely on Him always because I sometimes did not know how to narrate my thoughts. I realized that God was working on my confidence in Him and building my trust in Him. To God be the glory!

If God is asking you right now as you read this to do something that seems out of your reach or out of your experience, I would like to encourage you to step out in faith and trust that He will give you the tools you need to accomplish what He has called you to do. This may be starting a business, writing a book, starting a nonprofit organization, or something else. No matter what God puts in your heart, you must trust that He knows the end and has all you need to accomplish it. He will not ask you to do something that requires you to stay comfortable. He wants to stretch you and build your faith as you do what He calls you to do, so that the glory belongs to Him (2 Corinthians 4:7). Therefore, God wants you to remember that what He takes you through, as you step out in faith, is so that when you reach the finish line, you remember Him and share with others what He did through you.

When I started writing the book, I faced many fears. I was good at sharing my story with the people I knew, but I was not ready to share it with the world and have no control over who would hear it or read it. I was also afraid of how my family would react if I shared my story publicly, but I realized that God wanted me to write this book first so that He could heal some parts of my heart and take me into a complete walk of freedom. Also, God wanted to bring healing to many others, including my family. I came to see that my story was not about me anymore. Although I was afraid of rejection, I realized that the walk of Christians takes us through painful paths where we may face rejection. Therefore, God wanted me to live a life focused on fulfilling my purpose, just as Jesus did when He was doing His Father's will on earth (Luke 2:49), and not focus on what people would say or who may choose to reject me after I had shared my story. I learned to depend on God when I was called to leave my family and find myself in an unknown place relying on His guidance and favor.

Being away from my family gave me a new perspective of God and brought me to total dependence on Him. God promised us that we were not orphans because He is always with us and because through His salvation He has given us a family in Christ as it says in Mark 10:29-30. I encourage you to trust God and let go of any fear of rejection because Jesus is faithful to fill any void in your heart, to bring people into your life to help you fulfill your destiny, and He will make your walk less painful and more meaningful. Jesus promised us that we would face trials and tribulations (Luke 21:12-19) as we walk with Him. Therefore, we should take courage and trust in His unfailing love and grace to carry us through every situation that we will face as we step out in faith to do what He has called us to do.

Through my walk in writing this book, I was isolated from my family and could not see the people I loved. It was hurtful and hard not to think about them, but God gave me a revelation of the importance of peaceful solitude; a quiet place with Him, so that I could have my full focus on Him.

When you step into the purpose that God is reminding you of as you read this book, you should know that God may take you to paths that are solitary to build you and stretch your faith so that you may rely on Him. The path to your destiny is narrow and sometimes hard to walk. The enemy would always try to make you give up and stop walking. I encourage you to keep on doing what God tells you to do and trust in His unfailing love. God never says anything or orders anything that will not be fulfilled. He is faithful and will take you through any trial or tribulation and will use your story to affect many others. I encourage you to trust in Jesus Christ, the author and finisher of your faith, because He will never fail you, nor will He forsake you.

CHAPTER 2
A Child in the Making

My parents, John and Claudine, were born in Rwanda and came from two different worlds. My father was from a low-income family and my mother was from a wealthy family. In addition to their different backgrounds, my parents were from two different tribes. My father was Tutsi, and my mother was Hutu.

Rwanda is situated in the Great Lake Region in East Africa and has two main tribes: the Hutus (the majority tribe) and the Tutsis. At the Berlin conference (1884-1885), Rwanda was given to the Germans to be colonized. Nevertheless, Germany did not govern the country and gave the power to the Rwandan king, also called Mwami. After the First World War, Germany had to surrender it's colonies under the Treaty of Versailles in 1919. Hence, Rwanda and Burundi were given to Belgium. The direction of the Belgian power made the tribes distinct by looking at the physical appearance to distinguish between Hutus and Tutsis. This racist technique consisted of nose and skull measurements. The Belgian power instituted the mandatory identification card that would specify the tribe of each Rwandan based on external appearances and ethnic origins. In 1959, a massive killing of Tutsis caused many Tutsi families to go into exile in neighboring countries. Therefore, after this first attempt of destroying the Tutsi tribes, a genocidal ideology was taught to the Hutu people. Although the Hutu community was greater than the Tutsis, the Tutsis had a better trade system than the Hutu, which brought jealousy and hatred toward them (Haperen, 2012).

In the mid-1950s there was a move among the Rwandan population to request independence from Belgium. In 1957, a movement was founded: the MDR (the Party of the Hutu Emancipation Movement). This movement was founded in order to require the independence of Rwanda from Belgium and institute a Hutu government. When this movement was founded, the Tutsi community felt threatened since they were a minority, and the king who was in power was Tutsi. The king who was in power when MDR was founded was Muami Mutara III, and he ruled from 1931 until 1959. After his death in 1959, the Hutus rose in revolt against the Tutsis and orchestrated the first massive killing where thousands of Tutsis were killed. The Hutu revolt did not destroy all the Tutsi men before it was stopped. Rwanda and Burundi celebrated their independence in 1962. After independence, a Hutu leader was put into power, which brought more opposition and hatred for the Tutsi community (Haperen, 2012).

My father's extended family went into exile after the massive killing of Tutsis in 1959. However, my father's direct family stayed in Rwanda. Although the country was now independent after 1962, there were many limitations and much discrimination for Tutsis. In fact, it was hard for Tutsis to get scholarships and go to college. A few Tutsis were fortunate to study and work in the government.

In 1973 Juvenal Habyarimana came to power by a coup d'état and became president of Rwanda (Haperen, 2012). Under his authority, the ideology of the 1994 genocide against Tutsis was formed: a propaganda campaign with a main agenda to alienate Tutsis from Hutus. This propaganda was soon developed and put in the media and on the radio. The ideology of this propaganda had directives put in the "Hutu Ten Commandments." These commandments were as follows:

Hutu Ten Commandments (Haperen, 2012)

- Every Hutu should know that a Tutsi woman, wherever she is, works for the interest of her ethnic Tutsi group. Consequently, we should consider a traitor every Hutu who:
  - marries a Tutsi woman
  - befriend a Tutsi woman
  - employs a Tutsi woman as a secretary or concubine
- Every Hutu should know that our Hutu daughters are more suitable and dutiful in their role as women, wives, and mothers of the family. Are they not more wonderful, good secretaries, and more honest?
- Hutu women, be vigilant and try to bring your husbands, brothers, and sons back to reason.
- Every Hutu should know that every Tutsi is dishonest in business. Their only aim is supremacy for their ethnic group. As a consequence, every Hutu is a traitor who does the following:
  - makes a business partnership with a Tutsi
  - invests his money or that of the government in a Tutsi enterprise
  - lends money to or from a Tutsi
  - gives business favors to a Tutsi (obtaining import licenses, bank loans, construction sites, public markets, etc.)
- All strategic posts—political, administrative, economic, military, and security—should be entrusted to Hutus.
- The majority of the education sector—students and teachers—must be Hutu.
- The Rwandan armed forces should be exclusively Hutu. The experience of the October War has taught us a lesson. No member of the military shall marry a Tutsi.
- Hutu should stop having mercy on the Tutsi.

- The Hutu must, whoever they are, maintain unity and solidarity and be concerned with the fate of their Hutu brothers.
- The Hutu outside Rwanda must constantly look for friends and allies for the Hutu cause, starting with their own Bantu brothers.
- They must constantly counteract Tutsi propaganda.
- The Hutu must be firm and vigilant against their common Tutsi enemy.
- The Social Revolution of 1959, the Referendum of 1961 and Hutu ideology must be taught at every level to every Hutu. Every Hutu must spread this ideology widely. Every Hutu who persecutes his Hutu brother because he has read, spread, and taught this ideology is a traitor.

Therefore, in that period, because of these Hutu Commandments, it was hard for the Tutsi children to study or be part of the military. The Hutu government only allowed the brightest Tutsis to be enrolled in universities. Hence, my father, because of his great achievement in high school, received a scholarship to pursue his studies. He studied medical science at one of the best universities in the country and met my mother during his last year of study.

My parents were introduced by a common friend who happened to be my mother's late brother. My grandmother shared with me their story of how they met, beating the odds of being together in spite of the social limitations, and about how I came to be.

After my parents were formally introduced by my mother's brother, they soon realized they had previously met at the church campus where my father was part of the church choir. They continued to meet every week at church and started dating a few weeks after they were introduced. Many students at the time knew about their relationship, which was uncommon due to the cultural and social limitations.

My parents studied different majors. My mother studied agronomy while my father was finishing his medical studies and was about to start his residency. After graduating in medical science, my father was fortunate to start his residency in the same town he studied and where my mother was finishing her degree, which helped them to continue dating. As they continued to be a couple, it was surprising to many on campus who knew my mother's background and her family, but this did not stop my parents from publicly showing their love to other students and friends.

After many months of being officially girlfriend and boyfriend, my mother found out she was pregnant with me. Because the culture was not encouraging pregnancy before marriage and because of the difference of background and ethnicity, she knew it would be hard for her and my father, John, to be together. She decided to let her parents know before telling my father. She only told one close friend and asked him to pray for her as she shared the news with her family.

She invited her father and told him the news of her pregnancy. He was very surprised and asked her who the father was, and she told him the truth. He supported her, and her family started preparing for the wedding. Rwanda was conservative and did not want her to give birth before getting married. She told my father, and they prepared for their marriage, which was scheduled for July 31st, which happened three months before I was born.

My parents were excited to start their new journey as a couple and as a family. In addition to taking care of me, my mother finished her last year of studies and graduated after I was born. She had many dreams for her family and me. My parents both had many dreams, but unfortunately, they could not achieve them. A year after their marriage, my mother was killed in a car accident and my father's world was changed forever.

CHAPTER 3
The End of Clear Sky

On November 7, 1989, my mother woke up early because she had a trip to prepare for. She thought of taking me along with her, but changed her mind that morning and chose to leave me with my father. Because she did not own a car, she requested a ride from her close friend who was going in the same town. Her friend was a Catholic priest who traveled from time to time and would always take a few people with him who needed a ride. In those years, few people owned cars, and her friend was one of the fortunate people who owned one.

After preparing for her trip, my mother kissed me goodbye and left to meet her friend for the journey. She went to say goodbye to my father at his work and left with her friend. My mother had planned to go to another town and come back either the same day or the following day, which was the reason she left me behind so she could come back quickly.

On their way out of the town, they were hit by a truck, and my mother and her friend died instantly in the crash. This accident was written in newspapers and was said to be a conspiracy against my mother's friend who was involved in politics. Many who related the story said that my mother was in the wrong place at the wrong time.

When the accident occurred, people called the ambulance, and my mother and her friend's bodies were taken to the hospital where my father was working. He was told that an accident occurred, and his wife was one of the people who were killed.

My father was in shock, but decided to work and take care of his wife's body. Some relatives stated that my father contained himself after finding out the tragedy that happened to his family and prepared to say goodbye to his wife for the last time. He called both families and prepared for the funeral.

Since my father was part of the church choir, he decided to let the church know and went to rehearse the favorite songs my mother loved so he could sing to her at the funeral.

The family came as soon as they heard, and everyone was devastated by the unexpected passing of my mother. I was surrounded by many family members while my father was preparing for the ceremony.

Many people came to pay tribute to my mother and comfort the family for their loss. My father sang with his choir team and shared great memories of their short marriage. Everyone was very touched by the song my father sang for my mother and how strong he was when he said goodbye to the love of his life and the mother of his daughter. They were all shocked to see all he did for his wife's burial, how much he loved her, and the strength he had for the family and his daughter. The funeral was very sad as many who attended said. Many were astonished by his strength and courage taking care of his bride until the end. My father tried to be strong for me and shared that he would do his best to protect me.

After the funeral, it was time to restructure and find a new way to live without my mother. My father took many years to grieve my mother's death. I was always surrounded by family members and would go from one house to another for they all tried to fill the void that my mother left when she passed away.

My father focused on his career and devoted himself to taking care of me and meeting all my needs. Two of his close relatives moved in with us a few months after my mother passed away and helped him raise me when he would be on call for his job. His family encouraged him to start dating again and find a good wife who would take care of me, but it was hard for my father to think of replacing my mother.

My father decided to raise me in the same house he got when my mother was still alive and decided to wait for the right woman who would love me and take care of me.

Because of his determination and love for his job, my father became a successful and well-known doctor in town. He was promoted and given a chance to go to Europe for a conference, and he got an idea of moving abroad and starting a new life. He was determined to work hard and do all he could to give me a great future. He was not determined to raise me without a mother, but he was not in a rush to get remarried because he was still grieving the loss of his wife. My father never had to worry about my well-being. I was surrounded by loving family members and grew up surrounded by love.

People said that my father was my biggest fan. I was his beloved and was very spoiled by him. I remember times spent with my dad and how I would make him laugh as I sat on his lap to hear him sing to me. Even though my dad's career required him to be absent often, I remember my best days with him spent in laughter and filled with joy. Many who knew him told me that his focus was for me to have the best future and best mother as I grew up. He was determined to find the best wife and best mother for me. My father waited for four years before he started looking for another woman to be his wife. He did not want to replace my mother and took time to grieve her.

His friends described my father as a joyful and strong man who loved singing, loved God, and was always determined to help others. Knowing this, I was humbled and proud to have a father who lived a life that mattered until the end. My grandmother said that my father was not filled with hatred or resentment even when life was tough after he lost his wife. He always chose to see the best in people and give them the benefit of the doubt. Therefore, after hearing about my father's great qualities, I promised to make my father proud as he looks down on me and leave a legacy of faith on earth before I leave to be with my heavenly Father and my parents. These values became the core of my being. I learned to see life the way my parents lived and desired to share the love of God and love people in spite of their differences.

Although I did not grow up with my father and lost him when I was five years old, I kept a great memory of him, and his life shaped my personality and my beliefs today. I am so grateful to come from parents who were consumed with the love of God and people who loved each other with passion. Although I do not have a clear memory of my mother before she passed away, I am grateful to have had a mother who, according to her family and close friends, was happy to have me and excited to be my mother. I treasure the legacy my parents left in such a short amount of time. As I look at my childhood pictures and hear their stories from people who knew them, I see myself in both my parents. I am forever grateful for their inheritance and the love they poured into my life from the time they found out they were expecting me.

CHAPTER 4
New Life, New Hope, New Darkness

A few months after the death of my mother, my dad found out that his oldest sister was very ill. He brought her to his town and took care of her providing all the treatment she needed. Unfortunately, a few months later, she passed away. It was hard for my father and his family to go through another painful loss. It was particularly hard for my dad to go through another grieving season.

My father focused his mind on work and taking care of me. In 1992, he found that I was born with a deficiency on my left lung. My left lung was not fully formed, which gave me asthma and trouble breathing from a younger age. This condition was not common, and it was hard to find treatment or a cure in Rwanda.

After going to Europe for a medical conference in 1993, my father decided to migrate abroad so he could look for a specialist who could perform surgery on my left lung. He believed that surgery would give me more years to live; the current condition of my lung was not going to give me many more years.

After his trip abroad, my father told his family and close friends of his decision to relocate abroad in hopes of finding a cure for my condition. I was fortunate to read a letter he sent to a close relative where he stated that the best way for him to ensure I had a long life would be abroad. Many family members were not looking forward to seeing us leave the country, but they were concerned about my health and were willing to not have us close so that my father could find a cure for my condition. As I read the letter, I was so grateful to have had a concerned father who tried all he could to ensure that I would have a longer life than what was predicted. He was willing to leave his family and his country to live in an unknown place so that I could have a chance to have a healthy life.

The love that my earthly father gave me reminds me of the love of Jesus who was willing to leave His royal seat in heaven to come down and wear a corruptible body, to be mistreated, rejected, and crucified so we could have eternal life with Him and our heavenly Father. God did not want us to perish and sent His Son to bear the pain and sin for us so we may have eternal life. My father was willing to leave the job and notoriety he had in his town to go to an unknown place so he could give me a better life. It gave me more love and gratitude toward God who gave me a father who reflected His heart.

Before my father could start planning for our relocation, he met a lady who caught his eye. He fell in love with her and planned to marry her. Many who knew the lady and my father said that she was very loving and cared for me and my father. She was all that my father needed and he was excited to marry her and move to a new environment where he could start over again.

My father realized she would be a great mother to me. He wanted to raise me with a woman who would keep the same values he and my mother had, and love me as my mother did. After receiving many blessings from his close relatives and my mother's family, my dad proposed to the lady and started to plan for their wedding, which was scheduled for May 1994.

All the invitations cards were on their way before February 1994. My dad was very excited to spend the rest of his life with a wonderful woman who would love his daughter and care for him. He started preparing his house to welcome his future wife. He had been a bachelor for four years and asked two of his close relatives to move in with him after my mother passed away. It was time for him to prepare his house to feel like a family home for his future wife even though he knew we would leave shortly after their wedding. All my father's close friends and relatives were happy to see him excited for his wedding and could not wait to witness his big day.

The venue for the wedding and reception were booked; everything was going according to plan except the state of the country, which was about to turn into the worst darkness that could ever be imagined.

On April 7, 1994, the genocide against the Tutsis started in Kigali. Within a few hours, the country fell into darkness.

The atrocities did not start immediately in Butare, the town where we lived. My dad and his friends were given a chance to fly to Europe with their families for their safety, but my dad refused to leave because he could not go without his fiancée. She did not want to dishonor her family's belief and culture by running away with my dad without marrying him.

My father was not worried about being killed and thought his connections could protect him. Because he was a well-known and successful doctor, he had friends in both tribes and was respected. Because of his conviction and confidence in his relationships, my father turned down the offer to leave the country and decided to stay so he could protect his fiancée and her family if he had to. Unfortunately, nothing happened as he planned.

When the killings reached our town, my father was informed the following day that his fiancée and her family had been killed in their house. Alarmed and hurt, he ran to hide me with his neighbors. After two days in their house, my father resolved to leave the neighbor's house and go back to his house with the hope that his powerful friends would protect him if the killers came for him.

We left the neighbor's hiding place, went to our home, and waited for help or a rescue. Upon settling in the house, there was a knock on the door. Suddenly, my dad hid me under his bed and told me with a straight face to stay where he put me and not move. I was hidden under the bed and was terrified. I did not understand why he hid me and why his joyful expression turned very serious and alarmed. I wanted to call him back, but something in me told me to be quiet and wait for him to come back and get me. I had never seen his face that serious before. As a five year-old-girl, I just wanted to be with my dad and did not understand what was happening. My memory of that day was that I was dressed in my white dress and white shoes. I remember this because that was the dress I was wearing when I ran away and survived the genocide.

After hiding me under his bed, my father went to answer the door. There were three men standing with him and talking to him. I later found out that the three men were familiar with my father and came to kill us.

Two of the three men were arrested after the genocide and gave their testimony about what happened that day in the Gacaca court. The Gacaca court system was instituted by the new Rwandan government after 1994 to speed up the prosecution of hundreds and thousands of genocide killers who were waiting for their trials. The Gacaca court was mostly done outdoors in the grass, which allowed many witnesses to hear the details of the killers of their loved ones. I did not witness the trial of my father's murder, but one of my relatives was present and gave me the following statements.

In the Gacaca court, here are the statements of the two men, according to the relative who witnessed the trial. The two men stated that they knocked on my father's house, and when he came out, they told him that his friend sent them to kill him. When my father heard the name of the friend, he was reassured and asked them to give him a chance to write him a letter for they were good friends. They somehow agreed, and my father wrote a short letter that they took to the person who sent them. They were sent back a few minutes later to kill him. When my father heard their response, he gave himself to them. They killed him with machetes, took him out of the house, and left his body in an unknown place that we do not know to this day.

My last memory of my father was the time he put me under the bed and went to open the door. It took me many years to heal from the images I had of what I remember hearing while hidden under the bed. I remember how afraid I was when I stopped hearing my father's voice. I was scared to breathe. I thought my breath would make noise, and the people would kill me. I was paralyzed with fear. I did not move or close my eyes.

There was a deep silence in the house because they left with my father's body. As I was under the bed, I still believed my father would come back as he told me. My innocent mind believed my father would keep his promise and come back to rescue me. I wanted my father to hold me and tell me everything would be okay. I waited for him to come back and could not close my eyes or breathe out loud. I thought the men were still in the house.

After a few moments of deep silence and fear, I heard the same men who took my father away coming back in the house shouting. They came to look for me as they stated in Gacaca court. When they entered the house, I was frightened and could not breathe. I had respiratory and asthma problems.

One of them said, "Let us look for the little cockroach who might be here." They looked for me everywhere except under the bed. I believe God hid me. "For in the day of trouble he will keep me safe in his dwelling; he will hide me in the shelter of his sacred tent and set me high upon a rock" (Psalm 27:5). If you dissect this verse, you will realize that in the most troubled days, God promised us that He will hide us. That day was the most horrific day of my entire being. These men were coming to get me and give me the same torture they had given my dad a few hours earlier.

The men looked everywhere and did not find me, a little five-year-old girl, hiding under the bed. I cannot explain how they did not find me, but I believe God hid me and protected me in a way that I cannot explain to this day. I am forever grateful for His protection and believe that He sent His angels to protect me.

After their failed attempts to find me, one of them said, "Let's move on. If she's not dead yet, she will certainly die. We have more cockroaches to kill." They left and never came back.

I don't know how long I stayed under the bed, but I remember being thirsty and hungry. I fell asleep and woke up hungry. I cannot say if it was morning or evening, but I still remember the fear, hunger, and thirst.

After a long wait, I finally heard movement in the house. It was not someone who came to kill me, but was a family friend who came to see if we had survived the killings.

When she came close to the bed, I felt as if my heart stopped beating. I was frightened that it was the people who came to kill me. As she looked down, she saw me. She was happy to see me and with tears in her eyes took me out from under the bed. She had seen the blood at the door and thought I had been killed with my father. She held me in her arms and cried silently because she did not want anyone to know she was with me. She slowly put water in my mouth because I had no strength to drink on my own.

When I saw her face, I remembered her. My father used to take me to her house, and I knew her as an aunt. I was so relieved to see a familiar face, but I was too afraid to talk. I hugged her tightly and did not want her to leave.

After a long, silent hug, she asked me what had happened to my father.

I could not talk. I was still traumatized and could only recall in my mind what happened to him.

The lady gave me a banana and two steamed cassava. After I ate the banana and drank the water, we waited for the sun to go down. She took me to another house. I did not want to leave the house. I still believed that my father would come back and get me, but after many tears, she took me out. She took me on a bicycle, and we left the house. That was my last time being home and my last chance to believe that my father was alive. I was wondering where he was and if there was any chance of seeing him again.

After riding for a few minutes, she stopped behind a house. I was not familiar with the house or the people who were inside. As we entered, the living room was dark. It felt like there was no one inside, but we found many people hiding under chairs and behind curtains.

When the owner of the house saw us, he came and greeted us. She talked with him for a moment. Afterward, she came to me, knelt to be at the same level as I was, and said, "You are safe now. This man and his family will take care of you and protect you. I cannot come with you, but I know that they will protect you."

I cried as I heard what she said and hugged her tightly. She was the only person I knew after losing my father. I was sad to see her leave, but in my heart, I was still in shock about all that happened to my dad. All I wanted was to see him again. I did not know the family she left me with. Even though I was five, I could feel the pain and brokenness. I was very concerned about what was going to happen.

When the lady left, I went to the window and hid behind the curtains. It was dark, and no one could sleep. We were all petrified about what would happen if the killers came to the house. There was no light in the house. The owner did not want the killers to know that many people were hiding there.

I was hiding behind the curtain in the dark. I could not stop thinking about my father and wondering where he was. I was traumatized by the images in my head, but kept it in my heart. The family I was left with had four children and the wife was pregnant. I was now their fifth child. No one could cry because we were told to play dead, so that no one could hear a noise and come to look in the house. There were other families with children in the house. As I stood by the window, I heard a woman screaming outside. I looked to see what was happening outside and noticed that the house next door was burning, and the killers were standing outside of the house, shouting, and singing in triumph.

As the killers burned the house, they took a lady out of the house and threw her outside by the window where I was standing and watching. They tortured her and killed her with machetes. As I watched everything they did to her, more fear and trauma filled my heart. Before the lady died, she turned her face in my direction..

While watching what happened to the lady who lived next to the house we were hiding in, I thought about my father's pain. I could not stop wondering if the killers gave my father the same torture as the lady while I was under the bed. Since we were not allowed to talk or cry, I kept all the pain to myself, waiting to face to same outcome as the lady outside of the house. Two of the other children who witnessed what happened to the lady ran to their parents and hugged them tightly. I did not have anyone to go to because I did not know the couple I was left with. This made me miss my father more.

It took me many years to heal from the memories of the atrocities done to my father as I tried to find a meaning behind the pain. The memory of the pain and suffering stayed in my mind for twelve years.

After witnessing the death of that lady, I was shaken and was afraid of the thought that the people would come to the house we were in and do to us what they did to her. I could not cry or scream because the adults told us we had to be quiet so the killers would not come inside the house we were in.

That same night, the owner of the place we were hiding in decided that all the people in his house had to leave and run away because he was convinced that the killers would come to his house the following day. Therefore, when it was late at night, we all left the house and started walking. As we were walking, I fell and felt something under my back. It was not the grass or a rock. When I touched it, I saw that it was a corpse on the street. The streets were filled with corpses. I wanted to scream in terror, but I held my voice because I did not want the killers to find us.

We continued walking until the next morning and we saw a barricade of men armed with machetes in front of us. When we saw them, everyone wanted to run away from them, but we could no longer hide. We knew what would be the outcome of being found by them. They saw us from afar and were waiting for us.

As we walked toward them, every family was united in terror. I was with my new family. The father told me to say that I was his daughter, and I nodded. We walked slowly, and some women were crying and pleading for their children to be spared. As we walked toward the barricade, I felt no fear because I was ready to face the same treatment as the lady from the night before. I think my heart grew cold and I was no longer afraid of any outcome because I witnessed a succession of traumatic events. Although I was five years old, I knew the men were there to kill us, and that would be the outcome as we walked toward them. No one in the crowd told me that we were on our way to be killed, but fear and terror on the faces of the adults who were with us made me understand that we were in trouble. I was holding the hand of the boy who had become my brother.

When we got to the barricade, many men were holding machetes and waiting for us. As we got closer the armed men separated the Tutsis from the Hutu people who were running away with us because they did not want to kill their neighbors. While they were separating us from the Hutus who were with us, someone came and recognized me as the doctor's daughter. He knew my father, and he took me aside and hid me in a truck. I believe that man was not there as a coincidence. God aligned me with him so that I could be spared from the massacre. I believe God protected me so that I could live to share His goodness with you in this book.

After the man who recognized me left me in the truck, he went back to the line where my new family and the other people were waiting and started to put them in two lines. I could see everything from the truck just like I could see from the window in the house. I was filled with so much fear because I had gotten close to the family and the children who became my siblings. They were all standing in line and waiting for their execution. I did not understand why I was the only one to be spared. It did not feel like a blessing because I wondered why the man did not save the children and their parents because we were all standing together as a family.

One of the killers called out the pregnant woman who had become my mother on the side and threw her on the grass. This reminded me of the woman who was killed the night before. As the lady went forth, they tortured and killed her.

I was terrified to see what they did to the lady and tried to hide my face from seeing what they did to her, but I could not stop hearing her screams and the pain she faced. Although I had just met her, I had attached myself to her and her family. As a little child, I easily attached myself to people, and it was hard to understand that I would no longer have them with me.

The childlike, curious side of me did not keep me from protecting my sight, and I saw what the killers did to the lady. I witnessed her pain and the way all the people in the line were killed. I still remember the atrocity and trauma I felt when I saw the killers torture the people in unthinkable ways. I could not cry or scream because I was afraid they would realize I was watching them as I was waiting in the truck for the man who spared my life.

After a long wait that felt like an eternity of fear, the man who hid me in the truck came back and realized he could not hide me any longer. Therefore, he asked me to leave the truck and hide or else his friends would kill me. I did not get to thank him before I left.

After leaving the truck, I found myself running alone to a place I did not know. As I went, I found other people who were hiding and decided to follow them and go wherever they went. The killers were searching everywhere for any Tutsi they could find. We walked by night and in the morning we hid wherever we could find so the killers would not know there were more Tutsis alive.

When evening came, we could finally come out of hiding and start walking again because we did not stay in the same place twice. We ate anything we could find as we walked, sometimes going without eating, but nothing could stop us from running because we were all trying to survive. Although I was with other people, I was alone. I knew that everyone was running for their lives, and there were a few families who ran together, but I could not stop thinking about the first family I ran with and how they were killed.

After we walked for a few days, we saw a church in front of us. Every adult was excited and filled with joy. I did not understand why everyone was screaming and shouting when we were not allowed to make noise so the killers didn't find us. Then, I heard one of the adults say that we were now safe, and that nothing could happen to us. They all thought we could hide in the church and wait for the Tutsi army (Rwandan Patriotic Force) to save us from the killers.

As soon as we were close to the church, two ladies came out. They stood at the door and said, "Those who are Hutu should stand on the right line and the Tutsis on the left line."

I felt like I was living the same tragedy I faced a few days earlier when the family I ran with was killed.

We entered in the church and the ladies put us in a small room where we had to stand. We could not sit down because there were so many of us, and the room could not contain us if we sat. The only thing I remember was the smell of the room. I did not know why or how they could put us in such a small room, and many faces turned from joy to terror. No one knew what would happen because the ladies did not look pleasant.

Suddenly, someone took me out of the room in his or her arms. I do not know if it was a man or a woman. I don't know to this day who took me out of that room, but I believe with all my heart that God sent an angel to save me again from the massacre that occurred afterwards. I believe God kept His promises by sending His angel to protect me as He promised in Psalm 91:11 (AMP): "For he will command his angels in regard to you, to protect and defend, and guard you in all your way."

God, in His mercy for a motherless five-year-old who was about to find out she was fatherless too, sent His angel to rescue her from the massacre that was about to take place in that room. The angel took me out of the small room and put me in a latrine that was just a hole in the ground. I could see the defecation, and the smell was very disgusting since the toilet was closed and no air was coming from the outside. Even though the smell was unbearable, that toilet was my safe place. It became my safe place because I was not surrounded by killers. It was my hiding place from the killers who were looking to kill me and all the people I ran with.

In that latrine, I saw cockroaches in the hole and started to wonder why the killers called us cockroaches. I wondered why everyone had to be killed and what we did to the killers to make them want to torture us. I was not aware of the hate because I was just five, but I could not help but wonder why the killers had to kill children. During my run, I learned that I was Tutsi and had to run from the people with machetes and act dead whenever I heard them around. I was filled with immense pain and fear of the killers. I wanted to stay in that latrine forever. The smell was more bearable than the thought of being tortured with machetes.

A few minutes after the person, or the angel because I do not know to this day if it was a person or a divine intervention, left me in the toilet and locked the door, I heard soldier's boots. It reminded me of the incident at home with my dad. My heart started beating harder, and I feared breathing because I did not want them to realize I was in the toilet. They asked the ladies where the Tutsis were. They showed them the room where all the people were hiding. They went into the room and killed every person they found. People were screaming until there were no screams left in the room.

I heard the screams of the people and was horrified for the third time during my run. After they finished killing the people in the room, they were rejoicing with the ladies.

I was devastated and prepared myself to be next. I slept in the toilet and woke up more than once. I don't know how long I stayed in the toilet, and the only thing I remember to this day is the hunger and thirst. I was waiting for the ladies to find me and take me to the killers.

While I was in the toilet, no one came in, which was also a miracle to me. I believe God hid me again. How can anyone explain how no one came to the bathroom all that time? I was hungry, and I started to think of eating the excrement in the hole. You might think it was crazy of me to think of eating such a thing, but when you are in survival mode, there is no choice or reasonable thought. You get to the point where you might eat things you never thought you could eat.

Before I could start eating the excrement, someone opened the door and told me to leave immediately. It might have been the same person who put me there.

I left the church and started walking toward an unknown destination. I did not know where I was going, but I knew that I had to survive and run for my life.

I do not remember what happened after I left the church and started walking. My memory stops at the church. I am still praying that I will remember how I got to Uganda from the town I lived in, which was in the southern part of Rwanda. I found myself in Uganda, a northern neighboring country, and was placed in a refugee camp. I was soon reunited with some of my relatives. I believe this is one of the greatest mysteries of my life.

Although I do not have proof of my next statement, I believe God supernaturally transported me to the refugee camp where I was reunited with my grandmother and another relative. That was not a coincidence or could not be easily done. There were many refugee camps in Uganda, but God chose the one where my relatives were, so that I could be reunited with them and no longer be on my own.

CHAPTER 5
The Reunion

Some say that survival is a God-given gift; others say it depends on the person's determination to live. For a five-year-old child, I believe my survival was not due to my determination or my fight to live, but it was by God's grace and mercy that no one tortured me or killed me. It was with His protection that I managed to run for my life and live to testify.

To this day, I have no memories of how I got from the church to Uganda. I believe God either supernaturally transported me from the church to the refugee camp or cleared my memories of the trauma that may have occurred to protect me. I know it might sound unreasonable, but it is what I said to myself so that I could have peace to heal. I strongly believe I did not get to Uganda by accident or by my own strength and survival. The more I read the Bible, the more I realize my theory of being supernaturally transported was not uncommon. For example, Philip was taken away from the Ethiopian eunuch after baptizing him.

> When they came up out of the water, the Spirit of the Lord suddenly took Philip away, but went on his way rejoicing. Philip, however, appeared at Azotus and traveled about, preaching the Gospel in all the towns until he reached Caesarea. (Acts 8:39-40)

The first memories I had of my first time in the camp was seeing people who were injured and broken. I saw very injured children who were my age or younger than I was. The atmosphere in the camp felt peaceful and safe because I did not have to run or hide from killers.

The adults in the camp put us in a tent with many other children who had no one left. After a few days, I was reunited with my relatives and was happy to see familiar faces. As we were reunited, we shared our stories of survival and thanked God for being alive and together. I finally found peace and knew that I was no longer alone.

The genocide lasted one hundred days and ended in July 1994 when the RPF (Rwandan Patriotic Front) stopped the killings and saved the country. It was then time to count all the losses.

In the refugee camp, there were so many survivors. Everyone in the camp had a tragic and terrifying story. We could finally stop running, and could eat food, and drink clean water. That was such a blessing. I could eat again and take a shower, which was a miracle.

The one thing I remember most about the refugee camp was the state of the people. Many were injured and had bad wounds. We did not have a variety of food, but to me, it was the best food I had ever eaten because I had spent many nights without food. We ate a dish called *bugari,* which is made of corn meal, millet flour, or sorghum. This dish was one of my favorites since we were not given many choices. We also had sweet potatoes and porridge. The condition of the camp was not good in terms of sanitation, but to me, it was my shelter. It was the first place I found a sense of peace, and I could sleep again.

During our time in the camp, I got close to my grandmother. I knew that I was no longer alone because we had each other, but I could not stop having nightmares of all the things I saw during my run for survival. Night after night, the nightmares replayed all of the atrocities that I had seen, especially my dad's murder and the murders of all the people that I had witnessed. Many people in the camp had permanent injuries that were physical and easily noticeable. Some of us had injuries that were not physical, but were deep and emotional as they had more impact and pain than the physical injuries because it was not easy to find a cure for the wound. Some survivors had no legs or hands or ears, and I could see where they needed healing. As for me, I did not know where I was hurting. I just knew that I could not sleep at night and had nightmares. I did not know how to describe what I felt. The camp had many doctors and helpers who were helping the survivors. They tried to help as much as they could to heal and ensure that we were on the road to healing.

A relative was looking for any family member who survived. He was working for the United Nations (UN) and found out that we were all in the same refugee camp. He came down to meet us and got us refugee passports and plane tickets to a faraway country where we could live peacefully. We were all excited to leave the refugee camp and explore another country. A part of me was not excited because I still believed that my dad could be alive and would find us in the camp, but soon, my hope was lost.

After a few days, we left the refugee camp and flew to a country far from Rwanda with unknown expectations.

CHAPTER 6
A Strange Place

On November 3, 1994, my grandmother and another relative landed in a city in a new country that we would call home for a few years. In many ways the city was different than any place I had lived in: the climate was dry, and the people were different than the ones we lived with in the refugee camp. There were no tents or Red Cross trucks around us. We did not have to line up for food or line up to go to the toilet. The people around us were not physically injured or looking like they had been through painful events.

Even though it was dusty and hot, there was a sense of peace and a new beginning. As we arrived, we were reunited with close relatives who lived there, who were happy to finally see us since many people thought we had been killed in the genocide.

Although I was reunited with people who were related to me and happy to meet us, I was quiet because I did not know any of them except my grandmother with whom I traveled. There was joy on all their faces. My mind kept wondering what would happen to us because I was still in survival mode and traumatized from losing the people I loved. I had hoped that my father would meet us in the refugee camp, but my hope was lost when we left the camp and landed in an unknown place, far away from where I last saw him. That was the moment I finally realized he had been killed just like all the people I witnessed on my run to survival.

After collecting our luggage, we left the airport and drove to our new home. As I was looking outside the car window, there were new buildings and a new landscape. I realized that I was now safe and did not have to worry about men with machetes because we were far away from Rwanda. We finally stopped at a house, took our bags off the car, and went into the house. Many people were waiting to welcome us. None of us were in a real spirit of celebration because we were still traumatized from what we survived, and we were also tired after the long layover on the way. Only tears were coming down our faces. We tried to smile and meet the people who were waiting for us. We ate home-cooked food for the first time in a long time since we were coming from a refugee camp.

After the celebration, we unpacked and discovered the new house, which would be our home. I was told that I would be sleeping with two of my close relatives. They were also children, but they were older than me. We got to know each other even though there was a language barrier between us. Some people only spoke French, and I only understood the native language, Kinyarwanda.

We went to sleep because we were all exhausted from the long trip and all the sleepless nights we endured in the refugee camp. I could not close my eyes because I was very scared of the darkness and had the lights on the entire night. In my mind, I was replaying all the scenes I saw on my walk to survival.

My grandmother was concerned about my sleepless nights, but she was unable to help because she did not know how to make me forget what I had seen. There were not many adults in the house who had stable jobs, although there were fourteen people. It was hard to have extra activities, such as finding a therapist who could help me with the nightmares I had and all the vivid images I had seen.

The United Nations High Commissioner for Refugees (UNHCR), an organization that takes care of refugees and provides resources to facilitate the process of healing by providing counseling to help the traumatic state of the survivors, contacted the family and asked them the condition of the last refugees who arrived: my grandmother, a relative, and me. They told the institutions that I was having trouble sleeping and would always scream in the dark. I was also afraid of knives and other sharp tools that reminded me of what I had seen as I was running.

After many visits to the house, the UNHCR officers concluded that I needed a therapist to unveil the trauma I was going through and evaluate the level of trauma, so they could help me start the healing process. They wanted to make sure I could go to school and live a life of recovery.

A few days later, I started going to therapist sessions. In my own opinion, the first therapist did not do anything. As a traumatized child, I could not be in a closed room with any adult who I did not know, or share my story with people who I did not trust, because I was still afraid that people wanted to kill me. It was hard for me to go back to the painful memories that I witnessed with the first therapist since I did not know her.

Therefore, my first meeting with the therapist brought more fear instead of healing because I did not trust her enough to open to her. When she asked me to tell her what I felt, I did not say a word and completely shut down. After a few sessions, she concluded that they needed a better approach with me. They tried another therapist because she concluded that I was a highly traumatized child. She wrote in her report that I was too traumatized to go to school and needed more assistance. In the report, it said that I could not focus my attention on anything else as a result of the trauma that I suffered.

After my family received the report, my grandmother refused to give up on my condition and started teaching me at home. As she gave me attention and love, I started to see that I could trust her with my pain, and I told her all my nightmares. She always listened to my pain and promised me I would never be alone to fight against the bad people who killed my father. My grandmother became my confidante because we shared each other's pain as she told me her pain and what she had gone through. She also told me the story of my parents, how my dad loved me so much, and how I was my mother's treasure. The more I was with my grandmother, the more I felt better, and the more light was coming my way. I had hope that I would see them again after she planted the seed of faith in me. She always prayed for me and told me that my parents were watching over me, which gave me peace as I walked in my healing as a traumatized child.

The UNHCR decided to assign me to a second therapist for more sessions and counseling. They sent me to a man, and a woman who was translating what the he was saying, because I did not speak French at the time. We lived in a French-speaking country, and everyone spoke French as their main language. Therefore, the lady was translating what the man was saying to me in Kinyarwanda. These sessions were more helpful than the first ones. The man was kinder, and the lady who translated understood my trauma and fear of adults. I could remember most of my past and share it with the man and the woman after learning to trust them. That was not done in our first session. Every session was an awakening of many fears from the past that brought tangible pain and brought deep scars. I would spend my nights in my grandmother's arms, trying to hide and feel protected from the killers, because I always thought they were still looking for me and would come back for me.

After many sessions with the second therapist, I was taken to the final session by a family member. They wanted to find out if I was ready to go to school as a normal child. The therapist concluded that my healing should be done in an environment of love and care. He shared how the best approach then was to be homeschooled until I finally realized that I was out of danger and was safe. According to the second therapist, I needed to fully heal before I met other children or was in a new environment.

My grandmother was not happy to hear that I was not ready to go to school, and she committed herself to teaching me all that I needed to know so I could be ahead of the teaching when I went to school. I was sad to see the other children in the house going to school and coming back with homework while I was with my grandmother all day. When my grandmother saw that I was sad about seeing the other children doing their homework, she decided to give me more work so I could relate to them. She always reminded me of how intelligent I was because I had a genius dad and an intelligent mother. My grandmother always told me that I was not an ordinary girl and that I was intelligent, and that I had to thrive and always be ahead of everyone. I was reading and counting in French before I started going to school. I was too little to understand why she was always strict with me and wanted me to give my best in all that I did, but today I am grateful for her teaching and discipline because she made me seek excellence at a young age. I believe she saw something in me that no one else saw, not even the therapist who counseled me. She saw it and spoke it into existence. Today, I can still see it unfolding. She believed that I was special, and the Bible says that God handpicked us.

> *You did not choose me, but I chose you and appointed you*
> *so that you might go and bear fruit—fruit that will last—*
> *and so that whatever you ask in my name the Father will*
> *give you. (John 15:16)*

My grandmother had a revelation about me that I did not have at that time. It was revealed to me twenty-two years later when I started looking back at my past, the victories and the painful events that made me who I am today.

After the second opinion of the therapist, I realized that my grandmother had not given up on me. She was determined to make me move past my trauma and be a good student. She believed that I would realize the dreams my parents had for me someday.

A few months after the second conclusion, the UNHCR called me in and gave me a third therapist to see the progress and evaluate my current state. My grandmother asked to be in the room with me as the sessions began. My grandmother's presence gave me a sense of peace that I was not alone and could open to the specialist. The sessions were better than the ones I had before because my grandmother was with me. The therapist realized that I was more focused and answered his questions without any fear.

After many sessions, the therapist concluded that I was ready to go to school and face other children. I was so excited to see people other than my family and practice all that I had learned while I was being homeschooled. I was going to be the oldest student in my class, but I was not worried because I was ahead of my classmates because of what my grandmother taught me. I had started to speak French slowly and was able to write it. I was looking forward to being enrolled in a new school and having the experience that other children had. I was excited, but I was also anxious because I would meet other children. Nothing could stop my joy. For the first time, I felt like I was a normal child and could focus on my education and leave my pain and trauma behind.

CHAPTER 7
School Experience

After the conclusion of the last therapist, I was enrolled in primary school. I had to learn to speak French because I came only speaking my native Rwandan language.

Being the oldest child in my class made me feel insecure and lower than the other children. I felt that I was not intelligent enough to be with the children my age, and I felt excluded because I had no friends to play with during my first year. The language barrier was not allowing me to express myself and make friends. The other children had a different native language, which I did not understand, which isolated me, and they called me a foreigner. I felt lonely and rejected because the kids would laugh at my accent when I would ask the teacher a question. I felt rejected and denied the right to belong to any group of friends.

Fortunately, my grandmother always knew how to cheer me up when she came to get me from school. When I would see her at the gate of the school, I would feel safe and loved because she was the only adult who always believed in me. Every time she noticed that I was troubled by the behavior of the other children in my class, she would hold my hand and say, "Don't worry, Aline. One day you will be better than them, and they will come to you and ask to be your friend." Those words were reassuring and kept me going because I had hope that one day it would come to pass, and I would never be alone during break time at school.

Three years after my first day at school, I was used to being on my own and not having many friends at school. I had listened to my grandmother's advice and succeeded in my academics. I was now fluent in French and started to enjoy going to school. I made a few friends in my class and was more confident in speaking with people. Since my grandmother wanted me to be the best in all my classes, I was not allowed to bring home a low grade or even an average grade. She always taught me to be the best in every classroom. In fact, if I came home and was second in my class, she would correct me. This meant with a stick of my choice until I promised her I would never get the same grade again. My grandmother tolerated other children in the house having low grades, but she was strict with me and would correct me even when I had the highest grade in the house. I started believing that my grandmother loved the other children more than she loved me because she did not expect as much from them as she did from me. Many years later, I realized this was not the case because I saw that the rebukes and corrections helped me seek excellence in all my endeavors.

My grandmother believed I was smart because my dad became a doctor. According to her, my father was a genius, and she wanted me to walk in my father's path. She would not allow mediocrity in anything, certainly not in my grades. I was not allowed to watch TV before I showed her all my school homework (and the work she would personally give me to prepare me for the next lesson) was done. Although she was very strict with me, she always had a tender heart toward me. People said I was her protégé, but I could not see it when she was correcting me.

After succeeding in my first few years at school, my grandmother and her son decided to put me in a better environment. My uncle lived in a neighboring country and was willing to pay my school fees so I could attend a private school, instead of my being in the public school that was paid for by the UNHCR organization. My grandmother looked forward to having me in a better school because she believed I could achieve greater grades and have more opportunities to go to a better high school in the future. She was a visionary and always looked ahead.

After many family meetings, they decided that the best way for me to have a bright future would be for me to attend the best private school in the country where my uncle lived, and for me to stay with his family.

After applying to the best private schools in the city where my uncle lived, I was accepted to one of the best high schools.

That was a great opportunity for me. I could take better care of my asthma. The climate of the country we lived in was dry and dusty, which was not helpful for my lung condition because I was allergic to dust and many other things. My family believed I could get better treatments and have fewer issues if the climate was better than the one we lived in. My uncle was determined to find the best doctors to help with my condition as my breathing condition had worsened after the genocide.

After his decision to take me to his home, my uncle went back to start the process in order to bring me to live with him so I could start school a few weeks later. I was excited to be in a new country and meet new people. I was sad to leave my grandmother because she told me she would not come with me, but she promised to visit.

A few weeks later, my uncle came back to take me with him. I was very sad to say goodbye to my friends at school because I had made new friends there. And, I was sad to leave the children I was living with, but most of all, I was sad to leave my grandmother behind because she was the only person who truly pushed me and believed in me. She promised to visit me soon and told me with a strict voice how to behave once I got to my uncle's house. Although I knew she would be far from me, I was still afraid to let her down and not perform well in school. I knew that I would be in trouble, but I promised her I would be the head of my class and always let her know how school was going.

Before we left for the airport, my grandmother made sure I had all I needed to start school. My uncle told her how the school was very prestigious and how I would have a driver to drop me off and pick me up from school since my uncle traveled a lot for his job.

My uncle took me to the same airport where we had arrived a few years earlier from Uganda. I still had memories of our arrival in the new country I had called home for a few years now. I was very nostalgic because I missed my grandmother already and wished she would be with me for this new experience.

The flight was long compared to the one we had coming from

Uganda, which was a short trip since they were neighboring countries. As we arrived, I was amazed by the beauty of the airport, which was far more elegant than the one we came from. I loved the weather and the landscape of the city. My uncle told me on the way that he lived closer to the beach, which made me more excited. I had never been to the beach and was excited to discover it. My dreams as a young child were coming to pass. I was in a city that was not dry and had less dust, and I lived close to the beach. I had always loved water and was excited to see the beach for the first time.

We went home to drop our luggage before we could go to see the school I was enrolled in to start attending a few days later. Before we left the house, I was introduced to his wife who did not look happy to see me, but I was not focused on her. I was so excited to be there that I did not mind her reaction. The house had many rooms, and I finally had my own room for the first time. I used to share with other children or sleep with my grandmother, but this time, I had my own bed, my own bathroom, and my own study desk. It felt like a dream come true. I was amazed by the house and all the things I had at my disposal to succeed. My uncle had paid for all my books and clothes for school and was ready to show me my new school.

We drove from the airport to the school I was enrolled in. I was excited to see the building, which looked more beautiful than my last school. I could not wait to see how the school looked inside. I was astonished by the excellence of every place we went from the classrooms to the lunchroom. We met with the school principal, and he was very nice. He answered all the questions my uncle had and welcomed me to the school. I was given a school uniform and was told to come back in a few days. I was excited and could not wait to start studying at my new school.

After shopping for the school materials and books I needed, my uncle took me to an ice cream shop and got me my favorite ice cream: chocolate cookie dough. I was excited to see how I mattered to him and how he took care of me. We had a great time, and he told me that he was proud of my achievements, and wanted me to keep it up so I could be a great doctor if I wanted to be like my father. I did not know yet what I wanted to be when I grew up. He told me that my father would be proud of me if he was alive. He also shared funny stories about my parents. I was so happy to hear stories about my parents. It made me know how much they loved each other, even though they were together for only a short time.

We spent a few days visiting the city, and I learned my way around the house. Those were the best moments I had with my uncle. He told me not to worry about his wife and focus on my study when school started. I was excited to start school in a new place and could not wait to see how the children would react to me. I was not afraid to be alone and was ready to fight to be the best. My uncle was not able to take me on my first day to school because he had to travel for work, but he made sure I had all I needed before school started.

On my first day of school, I woke up with so much joy after speaking to my grandmother the day before. My grandmother was the best at cheering me up and making me feel unstoppable. She gave me more advice about how to act at home when my uncle was away.

However, due to trials and family matters, I did not go to school for three months and could not talk to my grandmother as I wished. I was mistreated by my uncle's wife who did not allow me to go to school. I was forced to live a painful life and could not tell my uncle the truth about my situation because he traveled for his work and was not around often. God intervened when my grandmother called the house and found out I was being mistreated. She came to rescue me. That was another season of traumatic events for me, but I am grateful because it taught me so much. I learned to take care of myself, learned to cook, I learned to clean, and to be more aware of the pain of others while I was away from my grandmother. Although this season delayed my studies, since I could not go to school as I wished, I learned many lessons that I still apply to this day.

My uncle apologized to me and my grandmother for the incident that I faced in his absence and he got us two flight tickets back to the country where I had lived with my grandmother and other relatives. My grandmother was upset at the situation and promised to never leave me again. I was traumatized and had learned how to keep all my pain within myself, when I did not have her around. Her presence gave me peace because I knew she would not allow anything bad to happen to me.

I started packing because I was leaving the following day and was relieved to go back with my grandmother. I had made great relationships with some workers in the house and was sad to leave them, but I was happy to leave the house that brought so much sadness to my heart. They taught me a lot and encouraged me not to give up.

I was ten years old when I went to live with my uncle, and I remember well the pain I experienced there.

My grandmother and I flew back to her home. I was going back with the one person I knew would protect me, and I believed I would no longer suffer because I was with her.

I was going to go back to school and wished to forget all the pain I experienced in my uncle's house.

CHAPTER 8
A New Environment

On our way to the airport, my grandmother informed me that she had moved out of the house we had stayed in before I left. I was not sad to hear that she moved out and did not mind being in any house because the only thing that mattered to me was being with her. She also mentioned that all the children who lived with me had moved in with a relative who was married and had a bigger house.

When we landed, a relative came to pick us up and took us to see the family member who all the other children had moved in with. I was excited to see my cousins again and was happy to be back home with my grandmother.

After we ate and played, the adults asked us kids to play outside as they talked with my grandmother. We had a great time, and I got to catch up with my cousins about school. They told me that a relative told them I was coming back and would be in the same school as they were. I was happy to know that I would not be alone and would have familiar faces in the new school. I was still traumatized from my stay at my uncle's house, but I was happy to be around the people I left, especially my grandmother.

After a couple of hours, I heard my grandmother calling me to come in. I ran to answer her. She looked at me with tears in her eyes and told me that I would be staying there for school. I was sad and cried as loudly as I could. I did not want to be separated from her again. I was broken and needed her presence to be healed. When my grandmother looked at me and told me I would stay with the relative, my heart was broken. As

I write this, I remember exactly how I felt when she told me. She held me tight and asked me to be strong. She told me that her house was not far, and I would always see her on weekends.

As a ten year old, I was angry at all the adults who made the decision, and I did not want to talk to any of them. They tried to explain how it was the best decision they could offer. The school they wanted me to go to was better than the one I went to before I left.

My heart was aching at the thought of not living with my grandmother and being with people I did not trust. I did not trust adults because of what I had seen in the genocide and experienced at my uncle's house with his wife who mistreated me, that caused me to think that all adults would hurt me. Although the adults were my relatives, I was scared of them because of what I had experienced, and did not trust them because I thought they would hurt me too. The decision to separate me from my grandmother strengthened my belief that all the adults present at the meeting were not good people, and I decided not to trust them from that moment on. Now as I look back, I realize their decision was not to hurt me, but was to allow me to be with other children and go to a good school. However, because of the events and pain I went through at my uncle's house, I could not see their decision as a good one.

My grandmother was a quiet and submissive woman. Although she knew I needed to be with her, she did not argue with her children. Therefore, she requested that I always be allowed to see her on weekends. They agreed to take me to her house every Friday. They also allowed me to stay with her until I started school, which was a relief because I wanted to spend time with her. Although she did not share her pain, I could see the disappointment in her eyes after the meeting. She tried to be strong for me, and she promised to always look after me.

My grandmother was my confidante, and not having her with me was always hard to take. I listened to her advice once again and spent the little time I had with her before returning to school.

One night, as I was spending quality time with my grandmother, she looked at me with tears in her eyes and asked me to forgive her. I did not understand why she asked for forgiveness because she had never hurt me and had always fought for me. I looked at her in great surprise and asked her what she meant. She started to share painful truths that no one in the family had ever told me.

She told me about how one of the fourteen relatives who lived with us when we came from the refugee camp was one of the three men who killed my father. I was shocked and horrified because I had been very close to the person she mentioned, and I had been sad when he suddenly left the country. My mind went back to the day my father was killed. There was so much pain, and my resentment toward every family member started to grow. However, my grandmother shared that no one knew until the police came the day after the person unexpectedly left the country.

I remembered how devastated my grandmother was when the police came looking for that person. No one told us why they were looking for him. I was putting the puzzle of my life together, and pain and anger were filling my heart. I did not know why my grandmother was sad that day, and I always wondered what made her cry at night. I could not understand why I lived for two years with the man who took my father's life and why I loved him as a family member. I felt numb to the pain, and my little brain could not comprehend it. Everything made sense, and I could finally understand why the atmosphere in the family changed after the police incident.

As she shared this painful truth with me and hugged me, I cried uncontrollably in her arms. I understood why she wanted me to leave the house and study abroad. I realized she did not share this painful truth because she was trying to protect me.

After our big night of truth, we tried to sleep and forget all we had shared. That night, I could not sleep because all the memories of my father and what I had witnessed came back. I kept screaming and waking up every other hour. I was so afraid. My grandmother prayed for me and held me in her arms as I tried to go back to sleep. The following day, she asked me to keep it to myself and never share it with any relative. She had been asked to keep it from me. I did not understand why I was not allowed to share it with my other relatives, but I obeyed her word and kept it to myself until I was twenty-one years old.

In addition to the revelation of who had killed my father, my grandmother shared more things she needed me to know. I did not understand why she was telling me all those things until she passed away a year later. My grandmother was a woman of strength and great faith. She always told me to pray for those who hurt me. After she shared all that she had to say, she asked me to forgive the people who hurt my father. He was watching over me from heaven. Even though my heart was aching, I obeyed and prayed for them. I believe my grandmother planted the seeds of faith, forgiveness, and prayer in me before her passing.

A few days later, I started school and went to live with the other relative. I was sad to leave my grandmother, but I was looking forward to our weekend visits. She always had a big smile on her face and would ask me how school was going. I always had to bring great grades to her because I did not want to make her angry. Although she loved me so much, she was very strict about my grades and my future. She wanted me to be a doctor just like my father. I focused on my studies and tried to forget about the painful truths my grandmother had previously shared.

However, there was more pain and more tragedies that came only a few months later. In August 1999, we were told that my uncle who had taken me into his house to study had passed away. It was devastating news because he was very loved, especially by my grandmother. We prepared for the funeral and flew to his house. My grandmother fell into a deep depression. I did not understand that she was depressed because I was eleven years old, but I recognized that her behavior changed. She lost weight in a short period of time and refused to eat or sleep. She lost her smile, and her joy vanished. I tried all I could to bring back her joy and smile, but I could not help her.

The funeral was very sad. Many people were grieving my uncle's sudden death. My uncle was a great man, filled with love, who cared for others. He was selfless and always helped everyone.

We stayed in the city where my uncle lived for a few days. It felt like a family reunion, and all the family was invited to say goodbye to my uncle. As children, it was always a great delight to meet close relatives who did not live in the same country as we did. They placed all the kids in the same room and asked us to stay in and play. We did what the adults asked and had a great time.

I could not help but think about my grandmother, and I wanted to see her. I tried to go to the room where she was, but the women with her firmly asked me to go back to the other room. I was sad not to be with her and looked forward to being in her arms.

When we flew home and I went back to school, my grandmother went back to living by herself. I always looked forward for Fridays because I would get to see her and try to make her smile, but she never regained her smile after her son's passing. She would spend all day in tears, and then cry throughout the night grieving her son. I tried to cheer her up, but I did not succeed. I lost my light and joy when she lost hers. She lost her appetite and could not keep anything in her stomach.

My grandmother was a woman of faith and would pray every morning and night, but after the death of her son, she lost the will to do anything. I was concerned about her and after our visits, I would always cry on my way back to my relative's house because I did not want to leave her alone. Her condition did not improve, and that was the beginning of tremendous pain for me.

CHAPTER 9
Beginning of Sorrow

After the death of my uncle in August 1999, a dark cloud covered my family. There was no more joy or peace in anything we did as a family. I went back to school and tried to concentrate on my studies so I could perform well and bring a smile to my grandmother's face.

Although my grandmother was no longer talkative after the funeral, she continued to share more information every time I went to her house. One of the most important conversations we had happened one day when I came back from school. I was about to tell her what happened, and she sat me on her bed and told me that it was time for me to be an adult and take care of myself because she would not be with me for much longer. I was shocked when she said that. I did not understand where she was thinking of going without me. I told her I would go wherever she went and would never leave her again. I did not understand what she meant, but as I recall that moment, I believe she knew that her time would soon end. She wanted to prepare me, but I did not take it to heart. I knew she was sad about losing her son, but I did not understand her words.

It feels like yesterday when my grandmother told me all the knowledge that shaped my life. At that time, I thought she was out of her mind because she was telling me what had happened in the past and what would happen in the future. I thought she was grieving the loss of her son. I realized a few years later that she was preparing me for her passing and enlightening me about what would happen to me six years later.

My birthday was approaching, and the relative with whom I was staying asked me where I wanted to celebrate my birthday. I asked for it to be at my grandmother's house, hoping that it would bring my grandmother joy again. My birthday was on October 20th, but we decided to celebrate it a week later because I had school tests that week. We invited everyone to come on October 28th to cheer her up. On the day of celebration, we went early in the morning to help my grandmother prepare for my birthday party. She was a great cook and would always cook for us every time we visited her.

Since it was my birthday, I requested my favorite meal, a Rwandan dish she loved making. She agreed to make it on one condition; that I had to be in the kitchen with her while she cooked it. I was happy to spend more time with her and watch her cook for my birthday, but I did not realize that would be the last time I would be cooking with her.

As we started cooking, she showed me in detail how to make the meal and reminded me of our conversation about how it was time for me to be an adult. I was turning eleven and thought she was not serious when she was asking me to be an adult at eleven. I did not take it seriously until later when I realized that it was the last personal talk we had together.

I loved cooking with my grandmother because she always took time to explain every step to me. As we cooked, I saw the happy face I wished to see on my birthday. She was more talkative and smiled a few times. I was grateful for the best gift I could receive from God by seeing her happy again. She was cooking for her family and friends, and she was doing what she always loved to do when the family got together.

Every time I closed my eyes, I saw my last memory of her making my favorite meal in the kitchen for my birthday celebration. She always told me to learn as she cooked because she wanted me to be a good wife someday and cook for my children.

After cooking and cleaning the house, it was time for the party. Many family members and family friends attended my birthday. I was excited to receive gifts and cut my cake. I was happy to see my grandmother talking to her friends and smiling. Many family members noticed her happiness and they were happy to see her as the happiest and funniest grandmother on my birthday. We all had a perfect day and great moments of playing and laughter.

Before the party ended, I was told that I would not be able to sleep over that night because the person who used to come to get me from my grandmother's house on Sundays was out of town and I had exams to prepare for the following week. Therefore, after cleaning the house and doing the dishes, we said goodbye to my grandmother. She was in her room with one of her close friends. When she heard I was leaving, her face changed and the sadness came back. I was sad to go and did not want to leave her. I hugged and kissed her good night. I did not know it would be my last time seeing her alive. We went home tired and slept in the car after the long day of activities.

We were dropped off at home, and the adults went out again. Later that night, Grandma called the house phone, and one of my cousins answered. She asked the cousin to give me the phone because she wanted to talk to me. When I answered the phone, she immediately told me to run away from the house I was living in because I would be mistreated if I stayed there. She repeatedly ordered me to leave as fast as I could. I did not understand what she meant because she had never spoken to me that way before. I called the relative who had answered the phone and told her what she said. My grandmother had said the same thing to her. This relative was slightly older than I was and she told me that our grandmother might be concerned about our well-being. She advised me not to share it with anyone, but to ask my grandmother about it the next time I saw her. We said good night to Grandma and went to bed since it was late.

A harsh hand woke me up; it was the hand of a family member. She looked at me with tears in her eyes and said, "Grandma passed away tonight."

I could not believe it and thought it was a nightmare that I needed to wake up from. I was screaming so loud that everyone came into my room and tried to calm me. They asked an adult to stay with us, and all the family members went to Grandma's house to figure out what happened and prepare for the funeral. The lady who was watching us asked us to go back to bed and try to sleep because the next day would be a long one for us.

I could not sleep. All I could think about was the last phone call I had from her and her warning to run away from the house. I remember her voice and how she sounded terrified and scared for my life. Therefore, I started to think she might have been killed. I was eleven years old, but I was wired to think the worst of people because of my experiences. I felt helpless and hopeless. My favorite person in the world was dead, and all I could think about was the fact that I was all by myself because I was not open to any other adult. I could not close my eyes without seeing her face and hearing her warning. I did not want anyone to touch me or tell me that everything would be fine. They did not understand who she was to me. No one could comfort me because my pain was deeper than I could explain.

I was rehearsing my last moments with her, recalling the words of advice she gave me after the death of her son. I could not stop thinking about the day she told me it was time for me to be an adult because she would not always be there with me. In fact, on the day of my uncle's funeral, after everyone went to bed, my grandmother told me that her time would come soon. She also said that I had to take care of myself and be strong because she would not be there much longer to protect me and take care of me. The cousin who witnessed my last call with my grandmother whispered in my ear and asked if we should tell our aunt what she had told us. I did not respond to her because I did not want anyone to find out about the call. I did not trust the people she had asked me to tell because of my past experience with them.

My grandmother always taught me to be discreet, especially concerning family matters. From the moment I heard she had passed away, I realized I was alone and had to fight for my life. I was cold to anyone who came to greet us or show support. I felt alone in the world; I was on my own. I could not find any peace in my heart. I hated the fact that I could not see her again and cook with her or listen to the stories that she only shared with me. And, I was angry at the family members who did not allow me to stay at her house after my party.

Some ladies brought breakfast and asked us to eat. I had no appetite and no one could make me eat or talk. I was thinking about all the things she told me about every person in my family. Nothing could bring any satisfaction or peace. I still could not believe that she had gone to be with my father and other family members in heaven. She always said she would one day meet my parents again and her loved ones who had passed away.

That afternoon, we went to my grandma's house to prepare for the vigil that was going to take place at nine o'clock that night. Her house was very clean because she always cleaned her house before bed. Many people were in her house preparing for her night vigil and her burial. As we arrived, we were asked to stay in her bedroom. We were all silent. I could still smell her perfume on her clothes and feel her presence. I held her nightgown and did not want to let go because I could feel her presence in the room. I remembered all the great nights we had together.

I felt a big void in my heart. I missed seeing her getting ready in her room. I realized she was really gone and I would never see her again on earth. I knew that I was alone, but I could hardly accept it. I thought in my heart that I would jump in the grave during the burial ceremony and be buried with her because I felt like my life was over.

I lay down on her bed, closed my eyes, and tried to sleep for a few minutes with her nightgown in my arms. I could not sleep for a long time because of the noise outside. People were coming for the night vigil and wanted to pay respect to our family. A tent was built outside the house to welcome all the people who were coming for the night vigil. People were waiting for some of my grandmother's children who lived abroad to come before starting the funeral and the night vigil.

After eating and getting ready for the night vigil, we were asked to go outside and sit with the people under the tent. Everyone was looking at us with sad and concerned faces. I was not looking forward to seeing my grandmother in the casket with no breath to hug me or talk back to me. I felt like I was in a nightmare and would soon wake up from it. Nothing seemed to make any sense. A few men brought her casket and opened it so we could say goodbye before the night vigil started. They let the direct family say goodbye and spend time with her first. We were escorted by a relative who did not give me much time to stay with her. They did not want us to be traumatized by her last image.

I do not remember how she looked in the casket. My last memory was from my birthday and how she smiled for the first time after her son's death. All I could remember was how I felt when she came to rescue me at my uncle's house. She promised to take care of me and never leave me alone. I never thought the day would come when I would see her in a casket with no life. I always had the assurance that my grandmother was always there to protect me. If she was alive, I had nothing to fear. With her by my side, everything felt possible. Seeing all the people lining up to say goodbye to my grandmother gave me great pain.

Suddenly a memory came to my mind. We were in the small house with fourteen people. I was coming back from school, and the rain was very heavy. I was walking home with my friends, and we could not hide. We decided to walk in the rain and get home as fast as we could. Since the rain was heavy, it flooded a canal. The water was flowing on the side of the road. Without noticing that we were running closer to the pit filled with water, I fell and the wind pushed me into the canal. The water had so much power that it quickly took me away. My friends felt helpless and rushed to get help. They found my grandmother and told her what had happened. She ran and asked a neighbor to help rescue me.

They took me out of the pit, and my grandmother was the first face I saw when I opened my eyes. I felt peaceful and safe; all my fears were gone when I saw her. This memory brought more tears to my face because I realized her presence always brought me peace and safety. Now there was no sign of peace or safety. I would be living with people I was not close to. I grieved and felt hopeless. I thought I could not survive without her. I believed nothing could ever bring a smile back to my face.

You may wonder how an eleven year old child could remember all this pain, but as a five year old survivor of the genocide, a part of my brain was wired to remember all the things I went through. I did not understand why until my salvation. I realized that God allowed me to keep all the memories so I could write this book. I pray that everyone who reads this book can find hope in any situation or tragedy. No tragedy or pain is too big for God to heal. Losing my grandmother was more painful than any other loss besides my father. I was so close to her and had learned to depend on her love and protection after the genocide. She was the only adult I felt safe around and I could always share my fears with her. I always knew she would help me.

The night vigil was very emotional and painful. The prayers and testimonies brought back many good memories of my grandmother. I could not stop thinking about her call the night she died. I did not understand why she told me to run away from the house I was living in.

We barely slept after the night vigil and we woke up early the next day to get ready for the funeral. We went home to get our clothes and get ready. I was still in shock and did not say a word on the way home. Many of my cousins tried to make me smile.

When they started the burial, I wanted to throw myself into the grave. Two adults stopped me. I was so angry and felt so hopeless. I saw no reason to stay alive. My parents were dead, and the only other person who truly loved me and showed me all I knew was going away to be with my parents. It was the fourth heartbreak I faced. The first heartbreak was the death of my father. The second heartbreak was the death of my uncle. The third heartbreak was finding out that a relative killed my father. After this last heartbreak, I felt I would never be whole again. I was eleven years old, and I felt like I had no hope and no future.

After the burial, we went back to my grandmother's house for the last time. When we went home, I went to my room and got into my bed and hoped to sleep and feel peace. Every phone call reminded me of my last conversation with her and what she had told me.

Every day was hard because I had no safe place to go. I was angry about waking up without my grandmother. I buried myself in my studies and focused on my future. My goal was leaving the house.

I will forever be grateful for all the knowledge and love my grandmother instilled in me. I miss her dearly, but I know as the Bible states in Hebrews12:1 that she is watching over me and cheering me on as I walk into my purpose to fulfill God's will in my life. She left a great legacy of faith in me, and I honor her and thank God for her. I will never forget the great lessons she taught me.

CHAPTER 10
Growth and Encounter with God

After a few weeks of grieving my grandmother's death, I went back to school and focused on my studies. Although my biggest cheerleader went to be with the Lord, I had promised her that I would continue to aspire toward excellence and to always be the best in my academics.

I finished primary school with good grades and started to apply to other schools. My family preferred for us to go to boarding schools because they believed that boarding schools provided the best education in the country.

In that country, every child who finished primary school would apply to three schools of their choice or the parents' choice. In my case, my first two choices were boarding schools. I personally liked the second boarding school I had requested because I knew many of the girls who were studying there. It was a safe choice for me and I would not be alone.

However, my family preferred the first boarding school that I had requested. It was the best school in the country for girls, and only bright girls were admitted. In order to be admitted to the first boarding school, you had to take an examination. Only 5 percent of the girls who took the test were admitted each year. I did not know anyone at the school, and I was not looking forward to being there. However, because of the great competition, I wanted to be admitted to the best school in the country for girls.

A few weeks after I finished primary school, I got a call to go for an examination at the boarding school that was my first choice. I was anxious and was given only a few days to prepare for the examination. A part of me did not want to succeed on the examination and be admitted to a school where I knew no one. However, because I never liked to lose, I studied and got ready for the test.

On the day of the examination, we arrived earlier than requested. I loved the environment and met two girls who were also very nervous about the test. We sat in the same classroom. The test lasted for five hours. At the end, I went home with hopes of being called back along with the two girls I met. I started to like the environment and the school more than I had expected.

After two weeks of waiting, we finally got the results. I was part of the 5 percent of girls who had been admitted to the school. I was excited to see that the two other girls had also been admitted. My family was excited for me and told all their friends about my success. We celebrated my success, and I prepared to go to the best boarding school in the country.

Several weeks later, I was ready to go to school. I bought all the things I needed for my first year (sheets, drawers, food, etc.). I was excited about leaving the house and being away from home. However, I was also stressed and worried about the unknown. I did not know any girls except the two girls I met at the examination.

On a sunny Sunday, my family drove me to the boarding school for my first day. I was excited to meet new girls and start high school. I was sad to leave some relatives who I had gotten close to after my grandmother's passing.

After unpacking and setting up my bed, I tried to find the two girls from the examination. One of the two girls was as excited and nervous as I was. After speaking to her, I went back to my dorm where I met a girl who was setting up her bed and drawers. Her bed was opposite mine. Her mother was very friendly and helped me get settled and put all my bags and clothes in my drawers. After her parents left, we started to talk and get to know each other. While we were about to go to sleep, we met another girl in our dorm. She was funny and made us laugh. I met many girls the first day at school and was excited about our new adventure. I became close to the first three girls I met. We were always together and shared everything.

A week after we started classes, the director came to our class and told one of our teachers to help nominate a class representative. My friends suggested that I volunteer because I would be a good candidate for the role because I was very expressive and verbal, and knew most of my classmates. I volunteered and was chosen to be the class representative, which was exciting and humbling. I could not wait to serve my friends and be their voice in the school. I had always wanted to lead. I was a leader in all my relationships because of my personality.

Although time had passed since my grandmother had passed away, my pain was still quite vivid and I was still filled with so much anger that it caused me to love fighting. I did not know how to express the loneliness and pain of missing my grandmother. I did not like to see people happy because my happiness had disappeared after the death of my grandmother.

I would frequently be involved in fights and then use my role as class representative to not get into trouble. I was angry at the world for taking my grandmother and my parents from me. I felt alone and not loved by anyone. My anger turned into bullying weak girls in my class and school.

On the outside, I looked strong and like I had things all figured out, but I carried a pain that no one knew about. I had dreams about my grandmother and remembered all the advice and secrets she shared with me. In order to hide my pain, I did not tell my friends that my parents had passed away when I was a little girl.

Moreover, I did not have the support I needed from my relatives. I decided not to focus on my studies for the first trimester and see if they would hear my message through my rebellious behavior. I was an angry and rebellious teenager, and I wanted them to see me and focus their attention on me.

I performed poorly with my grades for the first time and went home expecting that they would see my pain and get close to me, but they did not seem to care. I was hurt, but I decided to go back and study so that my grandmother and parents in heaven would be proud of me.

Not performing was not an easy thing to do since I was very competitive. I wanted to awaken my relatives by performing badly, but it did not work. I always wanted to be validated by them, but my wish never came to pass. I kept on trying until 2009. That was when I finally found my worth and love in my heavenly Father. He gave me the love of a father and mother. He is the Father of the fatherless (Psalm 68:5).

After our school vacation, with a broken heart and angrier spirit, I went back for my second year. I was determined to be the best since I was competitive. I went back to school with a determination to be the best for myself and no longer for them. I was very excited to see my friends and my teachers. I started to love the boarding school more than home because I found more peace at school than at home.

When I was admitted to the school, my relatives told me not to change my beliefs because I had been born Catholic, and it was an Assembly of God school. I was forbidden by my relatives to attend any service other than the Catholic Mass on Sundays. I obeyed the first year of school because I wanted my family to love me and be proud of me. However, after noticing their insensitivity, I started to reconsider all their advice. The school had mandatory services on Wednesdays, and they would invite a speaker. I went to the mandatory services, but I did not attend their Sunday services. On Sundays, I would go to a small chapel, and a Catholic priest would do a Mass for the Catholic students. I liked the Mass because it was quick, and I could go back to my studies and get on with my day.

When I started my second year, I got close to two friends who happened to be born-again Christians. I did not know this before we started to study together. When I found out they were Protestant (which was the name we gave to Christians who were not Catholic), I started to tease them and laugh at them. I was taught that Catholics were better than Protestants or born-again Christians.

Surprisingly, they did not try to argue with me when I told them their religion was wrong. They did not try to push me to change my perception. Instead, they loved me and always invited me to go with them on Sundays. I declined their invitations because I did not want to disobey my family's orders, and because I was scared that I would see their religion and love it. But, they did not give up on inviting me every time, and they would always smile after their service and tell me what their pastor had said.

I started to be curious about what they had experienced, but I was too proud to accept their invitation, because I did not want my Catholic friends to see me going to a Protestant church. However, there was a difference between my other friends and these two girls. They were more peaceful, and they were always joyful. I wanted what they had. I was an angry girl, and my joy was gone after my grandmother's death. I never knew I could really smile again and feel peace and joy in my heart.

On Sundays, the two girls would come to my dorm to get my friend (the girl whose bed was next to mine) for church. They would always invite me, and my response would always be, "No." I always found an excuse not to go with them.

Since the boarding school was a Christian institution, there were mandatory services for all students. Those services were weekly and were mostly on Wednesdays or Fridays. The director would have a speaker or visitor share the Gospel with us and have an altar call at the end of every service. The school had about 175 students, and a small percentage of the students were Christian. I was one of the non-Christians. Even though I was attending a Catholic church and going to Mass every week, I had no revelation about Jesus and had no personal relationship with the Savior. Therefore, I was not a follower of Christ, which is the definition of being a Christian.

Since weekly services were compulsory, I would attend and always raise my hand at the end of the session during altar call. I did not raise my hand because I was convicted of my sins. I did it to mock my born-again friends and their beliefs. I would always slander my Christian friends because I believed the only religion that was acceptable to God was the one that recognizes the Catholic pope, which was what my relatives had taught me. Every time I met a born-again Christian girl, a rage would rise in my heart. I did not understand why anger would rise and make me irritated about all the born-again Christian girls in my class. I had not read the Bible for myself and had never been taught to read the Bible at home. I was only taught to do the rosary and pray to the saints and to Mary, the mother of Jesus.

The anger and bitterness became tangible and noticeable to many of my friends and comrades, and they started to fear me and resent me. There was nothing that could bring me joy and happiness. I hurt some of my friends with my actions, my words, and my lack of trust. I hated myself for hurting others, but I did not know how to stop it or how to trust again. I was disgusted with myself and did not want to live. I had hurt the friends who loved me because I could not trust them enough to open my heart to them. I did not know that God had brought me to the end of myself so He could encounter me a few months later.

On January 25, 2002, we had a special guest who came to preach at our school. The director was excited to have him share the Gospel with us. Many people knew the guest speaker, but I didn't. My Christian friends were excited to hear him. I went to the service because it was mandatory. No one could stay in the dorms or do anything else. That day seemed usual to me. It was not my first weekly service, and I did not have any expectations for the sermon. I could not wait for it to be over.

After dinner, we quickly went to the great hall where the meeting would be to save good seats for my friends who did not want to be at the back. I went with them and was not excited for the night, but I was happy to go with two of my Catholic friends and two of my born-again Christian friends. The service started at seven o'clock as usual, and it was the praise and worship, which was my favorite part of the service. The atmosphere was peaceful and filled with joy. I was indignant at the meetings and never listened during the services, but that day was special. The atmosphere seemed different. Usually, I always mocked the gatherings and would be the last to go into the hall and the first to leave. But this service was different because I arrived early, and for the first time I leaned into the praise and worship for a little longer.

It was a special service because we had it on Friday instead of Wednesday. The worship was much longer than usual, and I was starting to feel a little peace as I was singing the songs. After the praise and worship, the director introduced the speaker and gave him the microphone to speak to us. I do not remember the name of the pastor, but I remember his sermon as if it was yesterday. I remember talking to one of my friends as the director was introducing him. A part of me did not want to be in the room, but I was curious to hear what he had to say since so many students were excited to hear him. There was a void in my heart that I did not know how to fill; as a teenager, I thought it would never be filled.

When the pastor went up and started preaching, for the first time in my life, I was drawn to the message. I listened to it, which I had never done before. I wanted to hear what he was saying. Normally, I would try to distract my friends from the preaching and annoy the other girls who wanted to listen. This service was different because I was drawn to the preacher's voice.

My friends were surprised to see me leaning into the message and listening to it without commenting on the speaker. The preacher's sermon was on Ecclesiastes 12:1-8. He started reading the verses, and one verse has kept my attention to this day:

> *Remember your Creator in the days of your youth, before the days of trouble come and the years approach when you will say, "I find no pleasure in them." (Ecclesiastes 12:1)*

A fear came into my heart, and for the first time, I felt like I could no longer feel the way I had felt before. I started sobbing, and the more he was preaching, the more I was convicted of my sins and in need of a Savior. My friends were shocked to see me crying and looking weak because I always acted strong and never wanted to cry in front of them. They did not know the reason for my tears, and they were concerned.

I felt like my life was worthless and had no meaning until then. I was running toward futile things that did not heal my heart and only brought more anger and anxiety.

The pastor talked about a Savior who loved us so much and was willing to die on the cross for us. I started to be curious about the Savior who the pastor spoke about and how He died because of His love for the people who hated Him. I started to wonder about the Creator mentioned in the scripture that the pastor read about in Ecclesiastes 12:1.

Before I could wonder more in my mind, the pastor mentioned John 3:16: "For God so loved the world that he gave His one and only Son, that whoever believes in him shall not perish but have eternal life." It was as though the pastor was in my mind and was reading all my questions because he answered them all.

He gave me all the answers I needed within half an hour. At that moment, I knew that I needed Jesus more than ever, and I wanted to know Him more and give Him my life. I was tired of running and not finding the love and peace I had always fought for. I could not spend another day without my Creator.

Before the preacher could invite people to the altar call, I stood up and went forward. My teachers and friends were happy to see me accept Jesus into my life. My two close friends, who were Catholic, joined me at the altar and we gave our lives to Jesus. That was my first time truly saying the salvation prayer and meaning it. Previously, I had said it as a sign of mockery, but this time I felt the supernatural power of God as I prayed when the pastor laid his hand on me. I felt the joy that my Christian friends had told me about. I felt alive and loved for the first time since my grandmother passed. I cannot fully explain how I felt that night, but I remember my spirit rejoicing and feeling renewed in Him. As the pastor touched my head, a new tongue was given to me. I started to speak supernatural tongues, and I did not understand the mysterious words coming out of my mouth.

I fell on my knees and felt renewed in God's presence. Nothing mattered anymore. I did not want to leave the hall, and I felt the peace I had always been looking for. After a few minutes, I stood up and realized the pastor was leaving. I ran to him and thanked him for praying for me. He laid his hands on me for the second time and prophesied over my life and my future. He said that I would be God's servant in many nations and that I would carry His voice to many lost people who would see the love of God through my walk with Him. I did not understand what the pastor was saying or why he said those words because it was my first time being given a word of knowledge. As he spoke, I was in tears as I listened to every word he said. The director told me to write them down, because they would come to pass.

I went back to my dorm in silence and went straight to bed. I did not understand what had happened to me or how my life had changed at the service because of my salvation and the prophecy the pastor had given me.

My friends came to my dorm, sat on my bed, and asked what happened to me because I had left them and followed the pastor to thank him. They did not see the second prayer he did for me. I did not know what it meant. I could not say a word. I cried because I was overwhelmed by the love of God and His forgiveness. I felt loved again, and I went to sleep that night with a heart filled with joy. My friends left and I went to sleep.

One of my close relatives had given me a Bible a year prior to my salvation, but I had never opened it. But on the day following that service, I woke up and opened the Bible because I was hungry to know more about Jesus. I did not know where to start, and I decided to start with the Book of John. I was hungry to know more about Christianity.

I went to one of the girls who I used to make fun of because of her faith. She was very devoted to God and was always kind toward me even when I was not nice to her. I went to her dorm to meet with her. It was Saturday, and we did not have class. I was scared to see her because I had not been nice to her and did not know if she would forgive me.

When I saw her, I apologized for my behavior and asked for her forgiveness. She looked at me with a peaceful face and said that she had forgiven me and was praying that I would encounter Jesus. I was shocked to hear she was praying for me in spite of all the things I had done to her. She told me she was happy and had praised God when she saw me at the altar. She knew our paths would cross for the glory of God. We started talking, and she taught me how to read the Bible by starting with the Book of John and reading through the Book of the Revelation, and then to read from the Book of Genesis through the Book of the Revelation. We decided to meet every night and pray together for our classmates and for the school. She was very determined to see the entire school filled with born-again Christians, and she was praying every night that God would bring salvation to all the students and teachers. According to her, being a born-again Christian was not a religion, but a relationship with Jesus. She desired that every girl would experience the love of God and develop a relationship with Jesus Christ.

I was hungry for God's touch and presence, and I read my Bible for hours. I started to find revelation in the Word of God, and I was determined to serve God with my life. He took away the old Aline, with all of her anger and bitterness. I was no longer slandering others or fighting with other girls. I started to love people and serve my classmates even more. I was nominated to be the class representative for the second time. My heart was made whole and I felt new. I started to intercede for my family and started to see my destiny unfolding as I read the Word of God. Many scriptures were practically fulfilled in my life as I started my walk with Christ:

- "I will give you a new heart and put a new spirit in you. I will remove from you your heart of stone and give you a heart of flesh." (Ezekiel 36:26)
- "Therefore, if anyone is in Christ, he is a new creation, old things have passed away; behold all things have become new." (2 Corinthians 5:17)(NKJV)
- "I have been crucified with Christ, it is no longer I who live, but Christ lives in me; and the life which I now live in the flesh I live by faith in the Son of God, who loved me and gave Himself for me." (Galatians 2:20) (NKJV)

CHAPTER 11
Beginning of Ministry

After a few weeks of diving into God's Word, my friend who had prayed for my salvation got a word from God to have a team of twelve girls, including herself, evangelize to our classmates and soon to the entire school. I was one of the twelve, which was a surprise. It was an honor to be with girls who had been saved years before I was. They were more comfortable using their spiritual gifts than I was. I was grateful to be given an opportunity from God to share His goodness with my classmates, and I wanted to serve Him with all my heart.

Every week, we were assigned a person to whom we were to pray for and share the Gospel. The twelve of us all had spiritual gifts of the Holy Spirit. In fact, every one of us had at least two of the gifts mentioned in 1 Corinthians 12.

I had the gift of speaking in tongues, and the gift of vision started to grow two weeks before I was chosen by my leader to be part of the twelve. Our leader had most of the nine gifts and was training us to discover our gifts and use them for God's glory. She was a prophet and was giving instructions for what God needed us to do. She was a prayerful girl who was always asking God for the next step to take and used the Word of God for every step.

We went in groups of two to evangelize our other classmates, and we met every Friday night to discuss our assignments and to pray as a team. The leader would give us new people to pray for and evangelize. I loved the Friday night meetings because we would pray for one another and practice our spiritual gifts. We always felt the presence of God in our midst. I felt more confident in my calling because I was no longer afraid. The team of girls believed in me and believed in the One to whom I had surrendered my life.

God was faithful to us and made us fruitful in winning souls for Christ. Within a month, we had won over all of our classmates for Christ. Since I was the class representative, I told our principal how we all had given our lives to Jesus. The director was grateful to God for the miracle.

As a class, we started praying for the other classes. Our lifestyle brought many students from other classes to Christ. After weeks of corporate prayers as classmates, we faced a terrible hardship that shook our faith. One of our classmates became very ill and was taken to the hospital in the city. After three days in the hospital, the director got a call announcing that our classmate had only a few days to live.

The director called me and shared the painful news with me. She was devastated and wanted me to know, to be there for my classmates, and to pray for our friend. I was shaken, but I believed that God could move the mountain in front of us. I asked the director if I could be the one who announced the news to my classmates. She agreed, but asked the principal to come with me.

On our way, she asked if I wanted her to talk to the girls if it was too hard for me. I told the principal that I was ready to share the news with my classmates since the Holy Spirit had asked me to be the one who announced the news. I did not shed a tear because God gave me the strength to believe that there was hope and a future for our friend.

I requested a meeting in the classroom. My leader came to me and asked me what was going on. She was the first person I told what the doctors had said about our friend's life.

She had faith and wanted to speak life to the girls. She was saddened, but trusted that God could do a miracle and change the story. We went to meet our classmates and told them what we were facing. The girls were terrified, and many were in tears. Before we could dismiss the meeting, we came up with a plan to pray and intercede for our friend's life. We all agreed not to have dinner that night and meet after our studies. We agreed not to eat anything until we could intercede for our friend. We tried to find a place where we could meet in private and pray together. We all started fasting as soon as we heard the news. Every girl was devoted to prayer. The principal allowed us to meet after 6:30 p.m. in the dining room. We went to the dining hall with the other students and waited for them to finish eating so we could prepare the dining hall for our prayer meeting.

Around 6:45 p.m., the principal gave me the keys to the dining hall. My leader went and called the ten girls who evangelized the school. When they came, we prayed to prepare the atmosphere before our classmates came. We covered the atmosphere with the blood of Jesus and welcomed the presence of the Holy Spirit. We felt the tangible presence of God and were confident that this night would be a miracle for all of us. After praying together, we went to get the rest of our classmates. The dining hall was filled with forty-two young teenagers who were hungry for God to move on behalf of our friend's life.

We started the meeting with praise and worship. After the worship, the twelve of us were divided in groups of two to pray for every girl individually so they could all experience the presence of God and be baptized in the Holy Spirit. While we started praying for every girl, some started to manifest a demonic presence and fell because the demons were uncomfortable in the presence of God. We were not afraid to cast out the demons because we knew the promises of Jesus for every disciple in Mark 16:17-18:

> *And these signs will accompany those who believe: In my name they will drive out demons, they will speak in new tongues, they will pick up snakes with their hands, and when they drink deadly poison, it will not hurt them at all; they will place their hands on the sick people, and the sick people will get well.*

It was my first time witnessing deliverance and seeing a demonic response to the power of the Holy Spirit. That evening, I noticed how powerful the name of Jesus Christ was. I lay hands on a girl who was oppressed, and I realized that when I said, "Holy Ghost Fire," the demons would be uncomfortable. The girl would try to run away from my touch because the demons were afraid of the name of Jesus Christ and the fire of the Holy Spirit. They would scream and try to fight us.

One girl started to push one of the twelve who was laying hands on her and calling the name of Jesus. When we heard the girl's screams, we all went and helped her pray for the girl and drive out the demon. We did not have any training for deliverance before that night, but the Holy Spirit gave us strategy and strength to overcome the fear and set our classmate free. The girl had so much strength that six of us could barely hold her. When God strengthened us, she was free from all bondage.

All the girls were amazed by the power of God. Many were baptized with the Holy Spirit and started to speak in supernatural tongues. We held hands and prayed for our friend as a family. All the girls could feel the tangible presence of God as we prayed.

As we were closing the meeting, the husband of our director called me outside. He was concerned when he heard screams, but I told him how the presence came down and delivered many girls and baptized them in the Holy Spirit. He was a pastor and thanked God for His power. He also asked me to be cautious during our next meeting. They wanted and needed to supervise in case there were strong cases that would be too hard for us to handle.

Everything went well that night, and we left the prayer filled with hope for our friend and knowing that God would move on her behalf. We also prayed for the school and the leadership. After we dismissed the meeting, the twelve of us stayed behind to cover the girls and pray together. We thanked God for His move in our midst. We went to bed and hoped to hear good news when we woke up.

The following day, I was called to the director's office. I was a bit anxious about what she had to say. The last time I was in her office, I heard that our friend was dying. I asked my leader to intercede for me as I went to meet her. She rallied the twelve and prayed for me. I went in faith, trusting that God would give me the words to say when I met with her. To my surprise, the director was smiling and asked me to sit down because she had great news for me. I was very excited to hear what she had to tell me. I sat down and thanked God in my heart for the news.

She looked at me and said with a joyful tone and tears in her eyes, "Aline, God has answered your prayers! Your friend is awake and healed!" As soon as I heard this, I jumped up from my seat and raised my hands in praise. I quickly thanked her, left the office, and ran to the dorms to announce it to the girls. I did not wait for the director to dismiss me and only realized it when I was already in the dorm. I told the girls the great news about how our friend miraculously woke up and was healed during the night. I told the eleven girls before telling the entire class.

We thanked God and decided to have a night of praise and worship. The eleven were very excited and thankful. Within a few minutes, the whole school had heard about the miracle and how God moved through prayers. We later found out that our friend opened her eyes around the time we were interceding for her in the dining room. We were all amazed by the faithfulness of God and how He heard our prayers.

This experience, and this great miracle, was my first time seeing the power of prayer and intercession. Our friend was healed that night, and many girls testified about healing and deliverance in their lives. To this day, as I write this, I remember that night as a memorial stone of God's faithfulness and power.

I am reminded of the story of Lazarus in John 11:1-44. I believe our faith as a team was strengthened when our friend came back to school. She told us how she knew we were praying for her because the Holy Spirit told her that this would be similar to when Jesus brought Lazarus back from the dead and brought his sisters to believe more in His power.

This miracle brought our class closer to God, and we all learned together to walk by faith and not by sight. We started to pray for other students in other classes. We had corporate prayer and fasted to intercede for our families, the school, and the teachers. We continued to share our testimonies and the good news of the Gospel with the new students. We were making disciples of Christ:

> *With great power the apostles continued to testify to the resurrection of the Lord Jesus. And God's grace was so powerfully at work in them all. (Acts 4:33)*

And God blessed us mightily and gave us success in our studies. We all graduated with high grades and received the highest scores in the country on our final examinations.

CHAPTER 12
Failure to Obey

Some of you can relate with me that sometimes it is hard to admit that we disobey God's Word in one way or another. In all honesty, I did not want to write this chapter because it shows more of my scars and my vulnerability to everyone. The Holy Spirit pressed in my heart to be honest and transparent with you by showing my flaws and sharing some of the vulnerable parts of my walk with God.

After giving my life to Jesus, spreading the Gospel with the eleven girls mentioned in the previous chapter, and leading the class to seeking God's face for our friend's healing, I was given an assignment by the Holy Spirit. However, I did not do it because I was afraid.

One evening after our prayer with the twelve, I went back to the dorm because I was exhausted. When I went to bed, I could not fall asleep even though I was tired. My spirit was restless until I started to pray and ask God why my spirit was troubled.

The lights were already off and everyone was asleep. I decided to take my flashlight and read my Bible before praying. My neighbor did not like the light that was coming from my bed and asked me to turn it off because she could not sleep with the light on. I apologized and turned it off. I decided to remind myself of some scriptures I had memorized that day.

As I closed my eyes to pray, I heard a tangible voice calling my name. I thought it was my neighbor who wanted something from me, but everyone was asleep. The voice was not the voice of a girl. I was afraid that someone was in the room. I started to pray in tongues because I did not know what else to do.

After a few minutes, I heard the same voice calling me again: "Aline, Aline, Aline." I decided to stand and see if someone was close to the door and needed help. I was afraid to see who it was because I had never heard the voice before. I covered myself with the blood of Jesus in case this was an evil spirit. No one was at the door. I called upon the name of God to protect the dorm and keep us covered in His blood.

After praying, I went back to my bed and heard the same voice calling my name for the third time. I remembered the story of the prophet Samuel in 1 Samuel 3:1-10 where Samuel was asleep and heard someone calling his name. He thought his teacher, Eli, was calling him. After the second time, Eli realized that God was calling Samuel and gave him instructions about what to do.

When I remembered the passage, I decided to do the same as Samuel did when Eli told him to go back to his room. I went back to my bed and repented for not recognizing the voice of God. I asked Him to come back and talk to me because I was ready to listen. I said, "Yes, my God, I am listening." After answering His voice, everything was still.

Suddenly, a bright light filled the dorm, and the place was brighter than ten times the amount of lights we had in the dorm. I was still in bed because I could not move my body. I turned my head to see if everyone was awake, but all my friends were asleep. I was the only one awake, but I could not move my body. I was amazed at the brightness in the room. It was brighter than anything I had ever seen. It was brighter than the sun at noon.

There was a creature in the room that was tall and had a white robe and wings. I was amazed by the beauty and peace that I felt when I saw the angel for the first time. It was my first time seeing an angelical being. There was a joy and peace in the room when the creature came close to me, and I knew it was an angel. I had read the Bible and I knew what angels looked like. It was an angel who came to give me an assignment. I had never had a heavenly encounter, but I felt so much peace in the presence of that creature. I remember the wings on the creature and the brightness of his garment.

When the angel came to me, he did not speak. He downloaded a message in my spirit. For the sake of privacy, I cannot fully share the message the angel gave me, but I can only paraphrase it. The angel sent me to a person to warn them about their actions and asked them to repent before it was too late.

As the angel download the message, I was shaken because I knew the person the angel was talking about because he had once visited our school. I did not know how I could meet him and tell him the word I heard. I was concerned because the angel had given a short time for the person to repent before it was too late. I replied to the angel's voice in my spirit (the conversation was not done in the physical; it was through thoughts): "How can I tell him this when I am in boarding school? Lord, please send someone else because I am too young and do not know your servant well enough to tell him these words. I am young and do not have enough experience or knowledge to stand in the presence of your servant and tell him what you have told me."

The angel replied, "You are not the only one who thought they were too young for the assignment I gave them. Jeremiah was young, but I still used him to do My will. As I was with Jeremiah, I will be with you. You are my prophet, and from this day, I anoint you to speak My word and bring the light to the nations I will give you. Fear not, Aline. I am with you."

That was the first time I was called a prophet and was anointed to speak the word of God. As the angel was answering me, I felt fire flowing from my head to my feet. I saw in an open vision, two angels coming down from heaven, and they clothed me in a garment. I found out later, that that was the day God anointed me for my assignment on earth.

I could not move, and I felt the tangible presence of God. I did not know what it meant. All of this was new to me, because I had never experienced the glory of God. I was at peace in the presence of God and did not want to leave. I never knew that I was a prophet of God, but I knew that the more God gives you, the more responsibilities you have (Luke 12:48).

I was filled with the fire of the Holy Spirit for the first time. I could see the angels worshipping God. I was in awe of God's presence, and I heard a song of worship. The room became brighter and brighter and time stood still. I wanted to stay in God's presence forever because I felt at home.

My friends did not wake up even though the room became brighter and brighter. After the open vision, I was moved by what it meant to be God's prophet. All the prophets in the Bible were rejected and persecuted. However, I was at peace about the future. I knew God was with me forever through the Holy Spirit. I do not recall how long the vision lasted, but it felt as though time stood still. I believe that once we get into the presence of God, time stands still because God is timeless.

After the vision, I fell into a deep sleep. I woke up the following day with an aching body. I wrote down the vision and what the angel told me to do. As I was writing, I started to doubt myself wondering how I could meet the person to whom the angel sent me. My heart was disturbed and I did not know what to do.

I was about to share my vision with my mentor, but the Holy Spirit told me not to. I did not know why I was not allowed to share my vision with her, but obeyed anyway. That was hard because I had shared all my encounters and visions with her, but could not do so for this one. That was a serious matter, and I did not know what to do or how to reach the person before it was too late.

The person who was mentioned in the vision was a relative of a girl in our school. I was not close to her, and I did not know how I could reach out to him and tell him what I heard.

We had three days to be home with our families. As I was packing, the Holy Spirit told me to go outside the dorm and walk toward the entrance of the school. I did not understand why He told me to do so, but I did it anyway. I went and stood at the entrance, not knowing why I was there. Some parents were already there to get their children. I knew my family would be late, and I was not in a hurry to pack.

As I stood at the gate, not knowing why the Holy Spirit sent me there, a person came to the gate. It was the individual the angel had told me to speak to. I was about to tell him, but I was afraid of how he would feel. He did not know me because I had only met him once.

I started to doubt what I had heard the night before. I made excuses for why I should not tell him. I was young, and he might think I was crazy. While I was trapped in my mind, he passed me and greeted me with a smile. I was afraid to ask him anything, and I chose to be quiet. I did not know how to stop him and speak to him. I went back to my dorm with remorse.

When I was picked up and went home, I was disappointed in myself. I thought about what I did not do and how I disobeyed God because I didn't trust myself enough. I was anxious about the consequences of my disobedience. I did not know if God would find someone else to accomplish the assignment I had failed to do. I could not enjoy my time at home because I was praying for God to have mercy on the man and send someone else because I was not worthy of the call. As I interceded for the man and for God's mercy toward him, I did not hear anything from the Holy Spirit. The silence in my spirit was hard to take. I had always had conversations with the Holy Spirit, but there was complete silence this time.

No one in the house knew I had given my life to Jesus and was no longer Catholic or that I would be baptized two weeks later. I was warned by my relatives before going to boarding school the first year never to convert to the Protestant religion. I would hide in my room to pray and read my Bible.

My weekend was not the best. I was stressed and anxious about what would happen to the man. God gave him a short time to repent before it was too late. I did not go out to meet my friends and enjoy my time away from school. I stayed in the house for the entire weekend. I was praying and asking God to give me a second chance to talk to him, but I was faced with complete silence from the Holy Spirit. I asked God to send someone else to speak to the man before the three days passed or to give me another chance to tell him. I was repenting for my disobedience and for not doing what the angel of God had told me to do. I was angry at myself and did not feel worthy of God's forgiveness. As I cried out to God for a second chance and for the man's life, I was faced with silence in my spirit, which made me feel bad.

When I did not hear a word from the Holy Spirit, I felt as though I had lost His trust and was not worthy of a second chance. I could not feel His presence the way I used to. I could not sleep that night because I did not feel any joy. My heart was aching about what I had not done. I did not spend time with the family. I went to my room and blamed it on the headache I had due to my weeping and prayers.

I used to watch TV every time I was home since we did not have a television at school, but that night was the first time I declined to watch TV. I excused myself and went to bed. They were surprised to see me sleeping on Saturday morning when I was going back to school the following day. A relative came to my room and asked me what was wrong. I told her I was stressed about the tests I had that week and that I had a headache. She closed my door and said good night.

I went to bed wishing God would have mercy on the man and send someone else to talk to him. I wished that the Spirit of God would speak to me again and give me a second chance. I cried out to God and asked Him to come into my heart. I felt like I could feel what Solomon said in Proverbs 1:28 was at work in my heart at that moment: "Then they will call to me, but I will not answer; they will look for me but will not find me, . . ."

Nothing could bring any joy to my heart because I felt hopeless because I had failed to act on the direction from God. I believed God would never trust me with another assignment or use me again. As disappointment came in my heart, the enemy came with his lies to make me believe I was a failure and would never hear the voice of the Holy Spirit again. My fears were louder than my faith. I cried so much that my headache worsened. I tried to close my eyes and find a way to sleep with a broken heart and a helpless mind.

I woke up the following day with a heavy heart, inner bitterness, and anger toward myself. I felt unworthy of being called a servant of God. I started packing because I was going back to school in the afternoon. I was asked to go to the Catholic Church with my family, and I had to go since nobody knew I was born-again. After church, we went shopping for food to take back to school. We could take some food after our visits home and would eat it for a few weeks.

I asked to be dropped off first so I could watch and see if the person would come back to school. When I got in my dorm, I unpacked my bags and went to the dorm where the relative of the person slept. Upon entering her dorm, I noticed she was not in her dorm. I was afraid to ask her friends where she was because I was not her friend. One of her friends asked me what I was doing in their dorm since it was my first time going there. She told me her friend was late and would be there soon. As we were speaking, the girl came in with her mother and sister. They seemed happy, which gave me peace, and I felt relieved. To me, this meant her relative was alive. I believed God gave him a second chance. I went out and waited for her family to leave. After spending time with my friends, I went back to the girl's dorm to talk with her and check how her weekend went. She was surprised to see me in her dorm and talking to her because we were not close. She shared her activities with me and how she enjoyed church with her family. I was relieved to hear that everything had gone well.

When I went back to my dorm, I was thankful to God for giving him a second chance. I was longing to hear God's voice again. I was grateful for His faithfulness, and was expectant of His voice. I gave thanks to God for giving the man a second chance.

The following day, the principal told me that they had bad news concerning the girl. Her relative passed away in the night from a heart attack. The girl's aunt was waiting to take her home to prepare for the funeral. When I heard it, my heart was shaking. I could barely say a word. I was excused and ran to the girl's dorm to see her before she left with her aunt. She was devastated by the news and was crying. I held her hands and prayed for her. I told her that we would pray and lift her family in their pain. She left with her aunt, and I went to the twelve to ask for prayer because I did not know what to do.

I felt destroyed inside and felt guilty for his death. I hated myself and could not forgive myself for six years even though God forgave me after I heard His voice again. Sometimes our greatest enemy is ourselves because we do not forgive our mistakes even when God forgives us. Although I was forgiven, I could not stop thinking about how different the outcome would have been had I obeyed.

Six years after the incident, God asked me to release myself and forgive myself as He had forgiven me. I was able to see God as the merciful Father who loved me in spite of my shortcomings and not as a bad parent who does not forgive a child.

After speaking to the girl, I fell on my knees and repented for my disobedience. I asked for God to forgive me and be merciful to me. I was hopeless and needed to hear the voice of the Holy Spirit.

One night, while crying out to God, I heard the voice of the Holy Spirit again for the first time in a very long time. He said, "Take your Bible and read Ezekiel 3." I knew this was not my own thoughts because I had not opened my Bible in a few weeks. I remembered His voice and how different it was from my thoughts. Many people may wonder how to differentiate their thoughts from God's voice. God's voice is a soft whisper, and as you read His Word in the Bible and seek His face, you will start to recognize His voice, your voice, and the enemy's voice. It is also important to note that His Word aligns with the Bible.

After I heard the voice of the Holy Spirit, I took my Bible and went to Ezekiel 3. A few verses stood out to me and brought the fear of God into my heart and spirit. Verses 17 to 20 shook me and were relevant to what had happened to me. The one describing my disobedience was verse 20:

> *Again, when a righteous person turns from their righteousness and does evil, and I put a stumbling block before them, they will die. Since you did not warn them, they will die for their sin. The righteous things that person did will not be remembered, and I will hold you accountable for their blood.*

After reading this verse, I was so scared about what I had done through my disobedience. The death of the man was on me, and I was accountable for his death even though I did not know him. I cried bitterly, asked for forgiveness, and felt guilty of the man's death. His face was in my mind for six years. I had no peace in my heart and could not sleep or study well. I was isolating myself from people who could see inside of me and who would ask why I was broken. I was ashamed of what I had done, and I felt no amount of grace would wash away my failure and give me the peace and forgiveness I needed. I loved God with all my heart, but I felt like an outcast from His presence and mercy. Although I received the scripture from the Holy Spirit, I did not allow Him to give me the understanding and revelation He wanted me to have. I allowed the enemy to bring more condemnation instead of listening to the One who gave me the scripture.

One Wednesday at church, a guest pastor was preaching about Peter's denial of Christ when Jesus was arrested. He started to say that Jesus had already told Peter at the Last Supper that Peter was going to deny Him three times, and it happened as Jesus said (John 18:15-27). When Jesus rose from the dead and appeared to Peter, He asked Peter three times if he loved Him (John 21:15-17). The guest pastor said that Jesus asked Peter three times to redeem the three failures he had when he denied Jesus.

When I heard the sermon, I was in tears. I asked Jesus to redeem me and give me a new heart to obey Him. After praying in my heart, I heard the Holy Spirit again. After a while, He said, "I have forgiven you, my daughter. Sin no more and obey me. Behold, I am giving you a new heart and a new spirit" (Ezekiel 36:26).

I could feel the presence of God again! It was an amazing experience. I felt His arms around me and His peace around me. My joy came back, and I could walk in confidence. I trusted that God had renewed me and given me a second chance. I was baptized in water a few days later, and I continued to walk in His guidance and grow in my faith.

A few years later, a similar situation was given to me. I had to say what the Lord had told me about the person. I was no longer afraid of what the person would say, and I wanted to obey before I could face the same situation. I went and told the man what the Holy Spirit told me. The person repented and was set free. Hallelujah!

My walk as a child of God and as a prophet has not been peaceful. It has brought hardship and rejection by many. Through my walk, I have faced rejection, persecution and betrayal in my relationships. I was desperate, and I wanted to be "normal" as the world defines. I felt overwhelmed by my calling, but God always reminded me that I was no longer living for myself. I was living so that God's light could be shown to the world. His light cannot be dimmed. I relied on God's peace and His Word, especially when the leaders of the church rejected me. I was always reminded of Jeremiah 23.

Today, I am thankful for God's gift in my life. I am honored to be used by Him as His servant and child. I do not like to give myself the title of a prophet because I believe the only title I have is "child of God." That's the title I will keep even in heaven. I am thankful for the mantle of prophet over my life. I still face rejection and persecution in my walk with God, but I take joy in the tribulations and hardships as James 1:2-3 states. I was reminded by the Bible that no prophet had an easy or peaceful life. I am ready to live a life that matters for Christ, and I am ready to face the pain and rejection with Him on my side.

I am sharing my story and walk of disobedience so you may know that there is no sin that can separate me from God. Jesus loves us so much and died for us while we were still sinners:

> *"But God demonstrated his own love for us in this: While*
> *we were still sinners, Christ died for us." (Romans 5:8)*

I know as many of you read this, you might feel disqualified for God's forgiveness and love, but I can assure you that Jesus does not disqualify you. His love is for every broken heart. As you surrender to Him, He gives you a new heart that would obey His Word and walk in freedom. When I disobeyed God, I disqualified myself because of believing the lies of the enemy. I allowed the enemy to give me an identity that was not mine, and I believed it for a moment. When I allowed God's Word to bring life to me by going to church, even when I could not hear the voice of the Holy Spirit as I was used to, God used the guest pastor to speak to my insecurities and pain so that one day I could speak to your insecurities via this book.

God is always on the other side of surrender. Even when you don't know how to come out of a life of sin, God can turn your life upside down and give you a new identity. He encountered Saul on the road to Damascus and changed his identity into Paul. Trust God even when you cannot see the light and He will always reach His hand toward you just as He did to me.

CHAPTER 13
Innocence Taken

During my four years of boarding school, I had good times and challenging times. I witnessed the power of God through healing, deliverance and the salvation of many. I also faced pain, loss, trials and persecution. At the end of the four years, I was sad to leave the place where I had met my Savior, Jesus Christ, and served Him wholeheartedly. I was sad to let go of my secret place; only in boarding school could I be a Christian without hiding my faith. At home, I had to hide my faith and follow my family's religion.

We had our final examinations and our class had 100 percent success. Our director was very proud of us and planned a party in honor of our success. She gave us many gifts and blessed us for the future.

I was sad to leave my friends and sisters in Christ. It had been a privilege to share the Gospel, especially with the eleven girls who became my family. It was time to bring out the light of Christ and share His wonders with the world around us.

At home, the atmosphere was not pleasant. Many things had happened while I was at boarding school. My aunt had lost her baby who passed away at birth. This grief was challenging especially to her and her husband. The state of the family was not improving, but worsened. It was hard to rejoice or to be united as a family without encountering arguments. I was always sad when I went home and saw the brokenness of my family, but I could not share the light of God with them because they were wary of born-again Christianity (to them Catholic was not a born-again religion). Therefore, the Holy Spirit asked me to be the light of Christ for them instead of showing the light of Christ to them, so that my behavior and lifestyle might turn their hearts to Jesus.

I started to intercede for all my family especially the couple I was living with. I faced many trials and persecution, but the grace of God took me through them and gave me the strength to pray for my family, even when my flesh wanted to take offense and not intercede for them.

A few months after boarding school, I started being sexually and emotionally abused by an uncle with the knowledge of his wife. It was a secret that was well kept within the family. I was young and felt violated by the people I trusted the most. That was a dark season for my faith because I felt hopeless and angry at God. I did not want to hear anything about the goodness of God because I did not understand why He allowed that to happen to me.

Just as many people do in times of trouble, I ran from God instead of running to Him. I was angry at God and thought He abandoned me. I thought it was His fault and that He could have protected me. But then, after coming back to Him, I realized that pain is never given to us by God. He cannot give what is not in heaven, and Jesus taught His disciples to pray:

> *"Your kingdom come, your will be done, on earth as it is in heaven" (Matthew 6:10).*

God only applies His will to our lives according to the heavenly realm:

> *He will wipe every tear from their eyes. There will be no more death or mourning or crying or pain for the old order of things has passed away. (Revelation 21:4)*

With the two scriptures in mind, we see that there is no pain in heaven and the will of God on earth is aligned to heaven. Therefore, God cannot give us the pain we experience. However, we cannot be exempt from pain and trouble in life. Jesus said it so well in John 16:33, that we will have trials and tribulations in this world, and James also encouraged us to rejoice in our sufferings (James 1:2). I believe that pain always has a purpose. Although God does not give pain to us, He does turn pain into purpose:

> *Not only so, but we also glory in our sufferings, because we know that suffering produces perseverance, perseverance, character; character, and hope. (Romans 5:3-4)*

Therefore, pain grows a person's character and gives them more hope. As we experience hardship and trial, we do not only mature in our faith, but we also relate to others as they walk in their path. We do not overcome any situation just for ourselves, but to help someone who might need an encouragement and have the hope that God would take them through their situation.

As I meditated on the previous scripture in Romans, I came to understand that God did not cause the sexual abuse and the pain that came with it. As I came to realize that God was with me through it all and never left my side, I ran back into His presence and embraced my freedom.

Losing your innocence at sixteen can bring confusion and shame. Your mind cannot comprehend the circumstances you face in the abuse. Because I was forced and had no choice, but to surrender to the decisions that some of my relatives made, I was confused and broken. I felt violated and had no place to run.

I was alone again, and I felt the same loneliness I felt when my grandmother passed away. The vow of purity I made to God when I gave my life to Him was taken away. I felt unclean and did not love myself anymore. I could not see what God told me I was when I dwelt in His presence. I felt far from God and abandoned in the hands of the devil. I would go to bed in tears and wake up in tears. My days were filled with darkness. I stopped reading the Bible and decided to live a sinful life.

I felt forsaken and denied the will to live a free life. It felt like living in bondage and not knowing how to be free from it. It is one thing when the abuse is done by someone you do not know or did not trust to protect you, but it is another thing when the abuser is a family member. I was regularly abused for three years and was afraid to share my pain with my friends. I thought no one would believe that the family member was the perpetrator. The abuser used fear and terror to hide the pain of what he was doing to me, and threatened me to keep me quiet around other people. Because of the fear and the fact that I believed no one would help me, I kept it in my heart and grew cold in my faith and trust in God.

During the three years of abuse, I did not say a prayer or read my Bible. I was angry at God because I did not yet have the revelation that God does not allow the pain in our lives and does not give it to us. I felt punished and rejected by family members, and I thought God had rejected me.

The enemy gave me a false identity that said I was ugly, unworthy, and unlovable. I believed it for three years as I walked in one of the darkest seasons of my young adult life. When the abuse started, I felt dead inside. My hope was lost, and darkness became my home. I felt violated and empty. Because my flame was dimmed, I did not know how to feel when I was with my Christian friends who still had the light of God.

The abuse was regular and would take place three or four days a week. The more I was sexually abused, the emptier and more hopeless I felt. The abuse was also emotional because I was afraid to tell people what was happening. I blamed myself for letting it happen. It is common for victims to feel guilty about the pain the abuser does to them, and I was one of the victims who thought I was abused because of my actions.

The abuse and secrets affected my relationships and my grades. I did not have any motivation to study or aspire to anything. I went from a prayerful girl to a sarcastic, hopeless, and negative girl. I had no morals, and I wanted to do all the things I had not done due to my faith and my beliefs. I started dating and tried to find my worth in all the forbidden things. I also isolated myself from my close friends who were still walking with the Lord because I felt unworthy of being near them. I did not want to go to church or listen to Christian sermons on TV.

After three years of sexual and emotional abuse, I came to the end of myself and contemplated suicide. The abuser would tell me negative things about myself. He told me the devil had already put the insecurities in my mind. He would pick on my skin, body, and shape, and used many painful words. Every day of abuse from him put me deeper into the hole of hopelessness and desperation. I started to hate myself deeply, and I wished I was no longer alive to hear him call me those names.

As you read my story, a part of you may relate to some pain you've experienced. People you trusted may have hurt you or spoke words that created insecurities that became a wall that prevented the light of God from entering your life. I would like you to know that there is no pain that the blood of Jesus cannot heal. I was broken and abused for three years, and I even tried to end my life, but God always brought someone into my path to bring me back to Him.

I would like to be the person who God has put in your life to bring you to His path. You may have never encountered the grace of Jesus Christ or been filled with His love and peace. It does not matter. If you are reading this book and believe that God healed me from all my pain, then believe that He can do the same for you too.

God is not a respecter of persons and loves everyone. You don't have to carry your pain any longer. You can just give it to Him before reading the next chapter. He is right here with you as you read this book.

> *"Come to me all you who are weary and burdened, and I will give you rest. Take my yoke upon you and learn from me, because I am gentle and humble in heart, and you will find rest for your souls. For my yoke is easy and my burden is light." (Matthew 11:28-30)*

Some of you were given a false identity that you believed all your life because of the things you went through. Your pain does not define you. Your true identity is found in God. God created you in His own image (Genesis 1:26). You are God's masterpiece. His works are always good, and so are you. You are beautiful, you are worthy, you are chosen, you matter to God, you are redeemed by God, and you are fearfully and wonderfully made.

Today is your day of freedom and salvation. You don't have to live in bondage any longer. Jesus wants to give you abundant life so you can thrive and live a life that matters. It is never too late. If you are breathing and reading these lines, God has a great plan and an amazing future for you. All He needs is for you to come to Him and lay down your pain and burdens. He will give you a yoke that is light and easy to carry.

CHAPTER 14
New Life

After three years of abuse, I was tired of feeling hopeless and unworthy. The devil started whispering in my ear that I would be better off dead, than alive. I did not entertain it at first, but because I was now living in darkness, I gave him the power to speak to my life. The devil only has the power we give him. The Bible says there is death and life in the power of the tongue (Proverbs 18:21). The things we say to ourselves are important because when we speak life, we give power to the Holy Spirit to move in our lives, but when we speak death or negatively, we give the devil the power to work in our lives.

I was running from the presence of God and not seeking His ways. I spoke death into my life and listened to the lies of the enemy when he described me in the way my God did not. I was overwhelmed with pain and felt unworthy of living. My heart was hopeless and darkness was hovering over my life. I felt dead inside and had no desire to live. I started to think about how to end my life. I thought God had abandoned me, and the only thing I had left to do was end my life.

In my first suicide attempt, I had all I needed to end my life. I got a rope and wrote a suicide note. I found a perfect time when no one was home to carry out my plan. After finishing all that I needed to do before I would end my life, a deep fear of God came into my heart.

Suddenly, I was afraid of missing heaven and instead experiencing eternal death (hell). I did not think about it before, but I was reminded that it was a sin to take away my life. Jesus came so that we might have life and live more abundantly. My mind went quickly to a verse I read when I used to pray and read my Bible: "The thief comes only to steal and kill and destroy, I have come that they may have life, and have it to the full" (John 10:10).

When I remembered that verse, I realized the devil wanted to steal my life and destroy my future. I threw away the rope and the letter. I cried bitterly, but this did not stop the feeling of hopelessness and worthlessness in my heart.

After I remembered the scripture, I did not pray or call upon the name of the Lord to rescue me. Although I had failed the first time, I still wanted to leave the earth. I continued to contemplate suicide. Suicidal thoughts do not leave easily, and we need prayer and counseling to be free from them. It is important to talk about it to someone you trust or call a counselor who can help you process the thoughts.

The enemy always attempts to isolate us and make us feel unworthy and alone. That was my case. I thought I did not have anyone to share my pain. I had gone so far from God that I believed He could not hear my cry, which was a lie. "Everyone who calls on the name of the Lord will be saved" (Romans 10:13).

This scripture does not say, "For the righteous who call upon the name of the Lord will be saved." It says *everyone*. No one is disqualified from calling upon the name of the Lord, and God will never reject whoever calls on Him or comes to Him. His greatest desires are to be with us and to set us free from all bondage. All you need to do is call on Him no matter the situation you are in and no matter what you did in the past. Jesus never chased away the sinners, but He loved them and set them free.

After a few days, when the suicidal thoughts came back, I planned a second attempt, which was to cut myself with a knife. I thought cutting myself would be easier than the first attempt, and I forgot the scripture the Spirit of God reminded me of the first time (John 10:10). As I thought about my plan, I was afraid of the pain and the blood that would come out before I died. That attempt failed too, but my pain did not go away.

The third attempt was to be hit by a car or a truck and killed instantly. I thought this plan was the easiest and most painless because the devil made me believe it. To me, that kind of death was not unusual since my mother died in a car crash. I thought it was better to leave the earth in the same way my mother did; instead, I would be the perpetrator of my death. It sounded right because I believed the lies in my mind.

My assignment was to find the perfect truck on the road for my plan to succeed. The day after coming up with my third plan, I had to go to a study group with my Christian friends. I tried to avoid them for weeks, but could no longer excuse myself from studying with them. One of the friends lived close to my house and wanted us to drive together. I declined her offer because I had another plan. I made up an excuse about why I did not want her to ride with me.

I had four friends, and two of them asked to come with me that day. I wondered why they wanted to come with me, especially the second one, since she lived far away from my house. After I declined my friends' requests, they suggested we all drive separately, but follow each other. I drove recklessly and looked for a truck to hit. When I saw a truck coming in the opposite direction, I was convinced it was the perfect way to die. I increased my speed as I got closer to the truck. I wanted to hit it and die instantly. When I was close to the truck, the driver pulled away and hit a pillar on the side of the road. I missed my chance to die. I was angry at myself for missing the truck.

My friends driving behind me witnessed what happened with the truck and rushed to check how I was. I did not say a word to them because I was angry that I had missed my chance to be killed. I felt like a failure and did not know any other way to do it because I was ready to end my life that afternoon.

When we arrived at our meeting, they confronted me. I told them what was going on with me and why I drove toward the truck. I could not hold back any longer and told them everything that had happened to me and how I tried to end my life three times.

That night was a turning point for my life because I finally opened up and shared what was happening with my close friends. They did not condemn me or judge me for my decision to end my life. They were all surprised to hear what had happened to me, and they were sad that I had kept it to myself for three years. They prayed for me and told me how much I mattered to them and, most importantly, how I mattered to God. They told me about how much God loved me and how He never left my side. They also told me about how they prayed for me even when I had isolated myself from them. That made me realize how grateful I was to have true friends who prayed for me even when I was not friendly to them.

I apologized for not trusting them with my pain. I prayed with them for the first time in three years. I closed my eyes and felt the sadness in my heart. I could not stop crying.

As each of them prayed for me, I felt overwhelming love and peace in my heart. I felt the presence of God just like I felt when I prayed before I was abused. I felt loved, protected, and surrounded by God's love. The presence of God was so tangible that I did not want to leave my friend's home.

After they prayed for me, I told them how I felt during the prayer and how the peace of God was back in my heart. I did not feel like God was far away, which I thought during the past three years. I felt renewed again after my friends prayed. I did not want to lose the joy of God ever again. They gave me all the advice they could, and they prayed for me one more time before we left my friend's house. When they prayed for me for the second time, the suicidal thoughts left my mind, and I never again felt the need to end my life. I believe that my friends were sent by God to deliver me from the suicidal thoughts and to put the peace and joy of the Lord back in my heart. I am forever thankful for these women of God who were used to usher me into my freedom. I love them so much and honor them with all my heart.

After their prayers and my rededication to the Lord, I was no longer afraid of facing the abuser and letting him know that he would no longer touch me or hurt me. When I left my friends, I went home and the abuser came in my room to take advantage of me that night. I prayed before meeting him because I knew he would come to my room and try to abuse me. When I faced him, I was filled with boldness and told him that he would no longer touch me. I was no longer afraid of him because I knew God was with me. He was shocked to see my boldness.

Therefore, he did not have any other choice but to leave me. God gave me the strength to face the abuser and speak the truth fearlessly.

That night, I cried out to Jesus for help. That was the first time in a very long time I cried out to Jesus and asked Him to rescue me. As I cried out to Jesus, I looked at the wall in front of me. I saw a man standing there and looking at me. The man was wearing a white robe with a golden belt. He looked at me with tears in his eyes, and He cried with me and felt my pain. I looked in His eyes and saw fire. Most importantly, His eyes were full of love for me. I saw Him, and I suddenly felt loved. I no longer felt alone. I was feeling the same tangible presence of God I had felt when I was at boarding school. When I saw the man in the white robe and the golden belt and fire in His eyes, I believed it was Jesus standing with me. I cannot fully explain how I knew it was Jesus, but deep within my spirit, I identified the man as Jesus. My spirit recognized Him as my Savior.

I fell on my knees and received the joy and peace I had craved for three years. I knew my Redeemer was in the room. He came to give me more abundant life (John 10:10). I was in complete surrender. He was approaching me and touching me. That was a touch that I had always searched for, but could not find: the touch of the Father. Jesus wanted me to be filled with joy, and He wanted to fill the void of not having an earthly father. I had a revelation that only Jesus could feel the void in my heart and no man could. His presence carried so much peace, and it filled my heart. Every part of my being praised Him. I was in the presence of my Savior, and I saw how He wept with me and saw the depth of my pain. As I immersed my spirit in His presence, I could not help but weep because I was undone. I asked Jesus to forgive me for everything I did when I was away from His will.

After pouring out my heart to Him for a long time, I felt His gentle touch. He said, "You are forgiven, my daughter. You do not need to earn it because I died on the cross and paid it all for you. You are redeemed by My blood."

As I heard His voice, I opened my Bible and read John 3:16: "For God so loved the world that he gave his one and only Son, that whoever believes in him shall not perish but have eternal life."

I felt so much peace in my heart when I heard my Redeemer declaring His forgiveness over my life. There was nothing else that held me back from experiencing the glory of my Savior. His blood washed away my sins and made me a new creation for His glory. I was no longer defined by my past decisions and sins. I was now defined by the precious blood of Jesus, which made me a righteous child of God. I no longer saw myself as a victim and as forsaken. I saw myself as a child of God who was worthy of love and fearfully and wonderfully made. After the restoration of my heart, the vision stopped, but I could still feel Jesus watching over me. I was no longer afraid. I fell asleep with so much joy in my heart.

I had a dream that night that I was walking by the seashore. There were footprints in the sand, and I was walking in the presence of someone else. I could not see the person who was walking alongside me.

When I woke up in the middle of the night, I cried out to God. I felt the dream was the description of the season I had been through. In my prayers, I told the Lord how alone I was for the past three years. I saw myself walking alone in a lonely place. According to my understanding, that was the meaning of my dream. I was convinced that I had walked through my pain, and the footprints in the sand were mine because I was on my own.

As I was crying out to God, I had a vision that was like my dream. I was on the shore, and the footprints were not mine. They were the footprints of a man, but I could not see His face. This man was holding me on His shoulders and was walking with me. This man had the same appearance as the vision of Jesus I had before I went to sleep. Jesus was walking on the sand and was holding me on His shoulders. Jesus had walked with me since the beginning and had never left me as I thought during the first year of abuse.

As I saw the vision and prayed for its interpretation, and a voice said, "Aline, My daughter, I was always with you in all you went through. I could not deny Myself, and nothing can ever separate you from My love."

The words in my vision were familiar. They sounded like scriptures I had read a few years before the abuse started. I took my Bible and looked for the scriptures aligned with the words I heard from the Spirit of God.

After searching for a few minutes on my own, the Holy Spirit told me that I could ask Him to show me where the scriptures were in the Bible. I asked Him to show me in His Word because I remembered how John Chapter 1 states that in the beginning was the Word, and the Word was with God, and the Word was God. I knew Jesus was the Word, and He could show me, with the help of the Holy Spirit who lives in me, where His Word came from.

When I asked, the Holy Spirit gave me two scriptures that I wrote in my journal and read later:

> *If we are faithless, he remains faithful, because he cannot disown himself. (2 Timothy 2:13)*

> *For I am convinced that neither death nor life, neither angels nor demons, neither the present nor the future, nor any powers, neither height nor depth, nor anything else in all creation, will be able to separate us from the love of God that is in Christ Jesus our Lord. (Romans 8:38-39)*

When I read those two scriptures, I realized they were exactly what I heard the Lord say when He spoke to me previously. It increased my confidence to know with assurance that God had spoken to me. It was aligned with His Word.

God still spoke to me even though I had not prayed for three years. I could hear Him, and I did not lose anything He had freely given me. I was happy to finally hear Him again.

The Holy Spirit said, "I was with you the first time it happened, and every night. I was with you when you wanted to end your life. I was the One who brought the fear of eternal death the first time you tried with the rope. I was with you the second time when I brought the fear of physical pain to you. I sent three angels to push back the truck from touching you on your third attempt. I am the One who allowed your friends to pray for you. Aline, I am the One who stopped the abuser tonight. I was in the room with you. I have always been with you. I cried with you and interceded for you. You were never alone. Even when you could not feel My presence, I was with you and holding you on My shoulder. Even when you were committing sins and doing all that was detestable to Me, I was always with you. I am faithful and cannot deny My child."

After He said those words, He gave me Proverbs 24:16: "For though the righteous fall seven times, they rise again, but the wicked stumble when calamity strikes."

I felt so much peace as I was reading this scripture. I also felt renewed and peaceful because I was no longer afraid of facing the abuser. I knew God would fight for me and would no longer allow the abuse. I did not fear any outcome because I gave all my plans to God and was ready to wait on His deliverance.

As I share my encounter with Jesus and His healing and restoration, I would like you to know that Jesus is there for you too. He never left you. You may be in the darkest season of your life and think Jesus is too far from you because He is holy, but I would like to encourage you and say that Jesus never leaves His children, wherever we go and whatever we face. We may try to run away from His love, but there isn't any place where Jesus cannot meet you. He is always waiting for you to call Him, and He will show Himself to you and give you the revelation of His amazing grace and amazing love. There is no situation too big or too bad for God to change. As God's children, we have the right to live a life a freedom. Jesus said that He is the way, the truth, and the life. Therefore, as He is the truth, when we know Him, belong to Him, and hold to His teaching, the truth will set us free (John 8:32).

If you are facing a situation and you do not know how to be free from or release yourself from abuse, addiction, or molestation, I encourage you to call upon the name of the Lord with all your heart and pour your heart out to Him. He is your deliverer and He will set you free from any bondage you face. I was in chains for many years and I thought the best way was to end my life. Even when I could not see clearly, God always protected me. He brought people to pray for me and intercede when I could not pray for myself. God used angels to protect me from crashing into a truck. He used friends who I thought would never understand my pain to lift me in prayers without knowing the situation I was in. Today, I believe God is using this book to let you know that He never leaves your side and is waiting for you to let Him in.

You may not know who Jesus is or have a clear revelation of His faithfulness, but you have faced many things in your life that made you question the presence of God and you cannot fully understand it. Some of the things you overcame were not due to your own strength, but were from God. As you read this book, you may relate to some of the seasons in my life and wonder how you've never identified Jesus.

As you read these lines, God wants you to know that the most important decision you can make is to call upon the name of the Lord. He alone will give you the revelation of your life and the purpose He created you for. God kept you alive this far because He has so much in store for you. He wants to give you an abundant life as you encounter His love and grace. There is hope for your future, and God will take you through your pain and turn it into a powerful testimony as you surrender to Him.

If you feel hopeless and lonely and think about ending your life, know that there is a Savior who died for you so that you would not experience eternal death. You can live an abundant life in Him. It is not over yet. You do not put a period in the story of your life where God puts a comma. In other words, God is not done with you and has a plan for your life. He will give you a life after your pain, just as He did for me.

The day after my encounter with Jesus, I went to school with so much joy, and I was no longer afraid to go home. When I got to school, one of my close friends who prayed for me the day before came to me and told me about how she was very touched by what had happened to me. She shared it with her father so they could find a way to help me get out of that situation.

At first, I was angry with her for sharing my secret, but when she explained why she told him, I realized she was doing it to help me. I remembered how the Holy Spirit told me He was the One who brought my friends to pray for me. I believe God was in control of whatever would happen. I apologized for being angry at her for telling her parents, and I agreed to meet them and share my story so they could help. Her parents were born-again Christians who loved me because I was one of their daughter's close friends. I was not afraid to share my situation with them. The Holy Spirit gave me the revelation of how the enemy wanted me to keep my pain to myself so he could have more power over me.

It is important to share what you are going through with someone you trust. It is not good to carry your burden on your own. The Bible says, "Carry each other's burdens, and in this way, you will fulfill the law of Christ" (Galatians 6:2).

We carry our burdens and allow others to carry ours too. It is important to have people you trust who can help you carry your pain. Of course, it is not wise to share your burdens with just anyone. Choose close friends who are godly and who can cover you in prayer. You need to surround yourself with friends who are spiritually strong. They will pour prayer into your life when you need it the most.

> *Two are better than one, because they have a good return for their labor; if either of them falls down, one can help the other up, but pity anyone who falls and has no one to help them up. (Ecclesiastes 4:9-10)*

It is vital to have friends and people who we can experience life with and lift up each other in times of need. God allowed me to choose the right friends in my circle before I went through the abuse. It was vital for me to have the right friends because I needed prayers and intercession when I was going through my dark season.

Even though I isolated myself from them and I did not share my burdens with them, they prayed for me and loved me in spite of my behavior. This is the unconditional love that only God gives to His children. Thus, it is important to align yourself with friends who will walk with you in all seasons of your life and still love you no matter what you do.

Finding the right people to confide in can be very hard because people may change in seasons. However, God knows the hearts of men.

As you seek Him, He will align you with the right friends who will lift you up and guide you in the ways you need to be guided. Friendship is important to God, and even when Jesus was on earth, He surrounded Himself with twelve disciples to fulfill His ministry.

As you read this, you may be aware that you have no close friends with whom you can share your burden. I would like you to know that Jesus and the Holy Spirit can be your friends right now. As you call on Jesus and pour out your heart to Him, He will carry your burdens and align you with the right people. He will order your steps and guide you to the people who will stand with you in all the seasons of your life. You are not created to live a solitary life. There are people aligned to you before you were born, and He will guide you to them if you trust Him.

My friend arranged a meeting with her parents a few days later. I went to meet them in peace because I believed God was working to deliver me from bondage. The meeting exceeded my expectation. I was surrounded with the love and prayers of many people who helped me carry my burdens. I was no longer fighting alone. Her parents took me to their church and introduced me to their pastor. He prayed over me with his wife. I felt overwhelmed with gratitude for how God raised so many people to stand with me and believe in a miracle.

After the pastor prayed for me, he sat me down and asked me to share my entire story. He sensed that I needed to pour it out. I shared everything without shame or fear. They all listened to me and some people were in tears as I shared my story. I could feel the peace of God in the room, and I was confident that God brought them into my life to free me from bondage. They asked me to come regularly for prayer so God could move on my behalf and set me free. They welcomed me into their church and told me that I was always welcome to be part of their church. I thanked the pastor and promised to come regularly for prayer.

After the first meeting, I felt a sense of peace. Although I knew the abuser might come back because I did not speak to him after the night I had an encounter with Jesus, I knew God would make a way for it to stop permanently.

The following week was my second meeting with my friend's parents and their pastor. After a long prayer session, the Spirit of God gave me the boldness to speak to my family and stop the abuse once and for all. Few relatives were aware of the abuse and those who knew did not stop it. I told the pastor and my friend's parents what God told me to do and the strategy He gave me for approaching my family. They all felt peace with the process and knew it was time for me to stand in the light and fight for my freedom. That was a critical choice, but God gave me peace. I knew He would go with me and would fight on my behalf.

I felt confident enough to sit down with my family and tell them I would no longer allow the abuser to touch me. The wife of the relative who abused me was aware of the situation and agreed with her husband when the abuse occurred. I decided to sit down with both of them and let them know my decision.

I had planned to leave the house later with a cousin who had also gone through the same pain and wanted to be free from the abuser. In fact, after the prayer with the pastor and my friend's parents, I decided to talk to my cousin. She shared her story with me and told me about how she wanted to leave the house and be free from the hand of the relative who abused her. As I listened to her, I decided to go with her. I requested a family meeting where we would tell them our intentions to leave the house.

The abuser did not know the reason for the meeting because we did not share with him in advance what we would talk about. This happened a few days after New Year's. Everyone was excited for 2008, and an uncle flew in from abroad to celebrate the holidays with us. The house was full of visitors, and no one knew about our decision to leave.

As I prayed for 2008, I was expecting to start my year in freedom. Because of the visitors and other relatives around, we asked the couple to have our meeting in a restaurant so we could talk privately. The uncle who was visiting was not aware of the abuse.

When the family members arrived at the restaurant, we started to share the reason for the meeting. I boldly stated everything God put in my heart with no tears and no fear because I knew He was with me and I would not put me to shame as I stood my ground. I faced my abuser and told him that he would no longer touch me because I would not allow it anymore. I told him that as a born-again Christian I found my identity in Christ and that nothing would stop me from living a life that was pleasing to God.

The abuser and his wife were shocked to see my determination and my boldness in sharing my faith with them. I knew they did not like born-again Christians and telling them about my faith was a bold step because I was aware of the persecution that could follow. I told them that I would leave the house with my cousin. I was ready to leave their house and be free.

God was on my side, and He gave me the strength not to cry before them like I used to do. They were shocked to see the change in my stature and personality. I used to cry at all the meetings, and I would apologize at the end of the meetings for the things they said I did. This time, I was not crying and I did not apologize to them at the end.

When the meeting ended, we went back home. However, I did not get to leave the house with my cousin because a family member asked me to stay in the house until I finished high school. I was about to graduate from high school in a few months. They thought the best way would be to stay in the house and focus on finishing my education. I would no longer be abused since everyone knew about the abuse.

Back home, we told the other family members who did not come with us about our decision to leave the house. After everyone heard the truth, the abuser was told not to touch me anymore and to let me finish high school before I left his house. I was not excited to stay in the house after I shared my decision not to allow the abuser to touch me. However, after praying and seeking godly advice, I agreed.

I obeyed the family's decision to keep me in the house until I finished my high school education and left for college. This was not the outcome I was looking for, but I decided to trust God. I knew that He would deliver me of the house of oppression in due time.

It was not a setback from God, but a setup to grow my faith in Him. As I look back at the things that followed the family meeting, God wanted to show me His power and how He could protect me from the relative who abused me in the same house where it happened. I was disappointed since my expectations were not met when I thought they would be, but I trusted that God would not allow the man to hurt me again. God kept His promises, and from that day on, the relative never abused me again. He tried many times, but God did not allow it.

I believed God was still in control in spite of the different outcome I was faced with, but I could not help thinking that this might be a trap set by the abuser. I was still living with him, and I knew he did not want anyone to know the pain he caused because he was a well-known man in the community. He was friend with powerful men in the country.

My decision did not stop the abuser from trying to take advantage of me at any chance he had, but God gave me the strength to fight back and show him that my mind was made up. He would try to come into my room, but I would never allow him to step inside. The Holy Spirit always gave me the boldness to face him and stop him before he could get in.

I started to grow spiritually and my confidence in Christ was growing. I was no longer afraid of him or any other relative. After their decision for me to remain in the house, I decided to change rooms. I did not want to sleep in a room that carried painful memories. I was ready to start a new walk with God, and I was no longer hiding my faith.

Although I changed rooms, the abuser would try to come and see if he could abuse me when no one was home. Because my new room was far from the abuser's room, and it gave me a chance to protect myself. Although he was stronger than me, God gave me the strength to stop him from entering my room. Whenever he tried to enter and abuse me, God's boldness became my personality. I was willing to face death, but not fall into bondage again. I knew God would save me from him if I stood firm and trusted God to win the battle. That season made me acknowledge that as God takes us into a season of healing, He shows His love and grace, which gives us the boldness to fight for it.

The harassment was increasing every day, but my faith in God was strengthened even more. None of the attempts succeeded. God sent His angels around me, and the presence of God was with me wherever I went. Although I did not understand the trials I faced, I believed God would deliver me someday.

One night, I was deeply asleep and did not hear the abuser coming in. He climbed on top of me and tried to abuse me. I screamed, "Jesus!"

at the top of my lungs, and I looked into his eyes and told him that he would have to kill me first if he wanted me to defile my body. "My body belongs to Jesus Christ!" I said it with no fear because God was with me.

When he heard this, he immediately stood up and left my room. After that incident, he realized I was no longer the girl he knew and had abused for three years. I was now a determined girl who would not give in to his attempts. During that season, I gained supernatural strength from the Word of God.

After the people I lived with found out I was no longer Catholic, they prevented me from attending a born-again church on Sundays. In the country I lived, some believed there was a difference between the Catholic people and born-again Christians which is the reason I am mentioning the different term. I would wake up early on Sunday mornings and listen to sermons on TV before they woke up.

They realized I was changing and was no longer drinking alcohol or doing the things I did when I was not serving God in my dark season. They decided to look closely at everything I did, and they went through my room to see what I was hiding. They found nothing because I carried my Bible and my journal wherever I went.

After their unfruitful search, they decided to stop me from watching sermons on TV. I did not argue with their decision because the Holy Spirit told me not to say a word. Since they realized I was waking up early in the morning to watch the sermon, they asked me to clean their house and cook for them since their maid did not work on Sundays. I would wake up to clean, cook, and take care of whatever they needed me to do before I studied. I prayed to God for patience and obedience to face them. I asked God to show His light in everything I did for them. I tried to be obedient to them, and I prayed for them so the enemy would not have a foothold in my life (Ephesians 4:27).

Some days were harder than others because I had to do the housework and study. I was in the final months of high school, and I had to work harder to earn good grades and be admitted to the best universities abroad.

I had wanted to study hydrogeology from the age of fourteen, and I was looking for universities outside the country so I could escape and live a free life where I did not have to sleep with one eye open. I wanted to leave the house and be the best I could be to honor my grandmother's wishes for me.

I decided to work harder, and I pushed for better grades. I was thankful for the support of my friends and their families. Sometimes, I would hide and go to church when my family was out of town. I started to get my life back, and I was growing in the Word of God.

I was at peace with any outcome because I knew God was fighting for me. The promise of God to deliver me from the house came three years after I told them my decision to end the abuse. Those three years were filled with persecution, rejection, and pain. Even though I did not see any outcome or know when it would come to pass, I did not give up. I trusted that God would keep His promises.

Every time doubt tried to come into my mind and make me question the work of God, I was reminded of Proverbs 19:21: "Many are the plans in a person's heart, but it is the Lord's purpose that prevails." It reminded me that God's purpose will always prevail in my life in spite of all the pain that men can cause in my life. I was confident that God would free me from the house where I had lost my innocence.

God always frees us from bondage in His own timing, but the process is sometimes different from what we expect. We may be in a process of freedom and transformation, and it feels like a delay. I always picture how a caterpillar has the potential to be a butterfly, but it needs to reach the stage of a butterfly first through the process. Although it is easy to understand this concept when it comes to development or growth, I believe this can occur in the process of healing and deliverance.

Salvation is an instant thing that we receive when we believe that Jesus Christ is Lord, but walking in freedom from bondage requires time. Many people give up because they are expecting a quick fix. God wants to give us life and life more abundantly by healing every layer of our pain. This process can take more time than we expect, but the outcome is worth the wait.

It was not easy to believe that God kept me in the house of oppression even after I repented and trusted Him to face my family and share the truth. It required me to lean on Him and allow Him to heal every layer of my heart and walk in total freedom once He freed me from the house.

I did not welcome the process with open arms. I cried many nights and felt defeated at times. Just as Jesus had to face the pain of the cross and be in the grave for three days, when it looked like He was defeated, there was a miracle in disguise. The disciples only saw Him when He rose after three days. I believe God allowed me to stay in the house and face many trials and tribulations while I waited for my deliverance so I could share with you and proclaim His faithfulness. God is never late and is always working in perfect time.

As you read this, if you are in a season of waiting for your freedom or your breakthrough, I would encourage you to wait patiently and trust Him to heal you so you can walk in total freedom. Your day of breakthrough will surely come, but I believe God is taking you into this season so that you rely on Him and He can heal you from any wounds.

God has not forgotten about you, and He is watching over you. Do not let the devil steal your joy. God is at work in your life even when you cannot see Him. He is building your character so you can be a blessing to others when He takes you through it. The people of Israel were not delivered at first. There were many plagues that came on the Egyptians before Pharaoh would release them to worship God. The Bible says that God hardened Pharaoh's heart (Exodus 9:12) and did not allow him to grant Moses's request the first time. God brought ten plagues on the Egyptians before Pharaoh would let them go. These plagues were brought so that the Israelites would not leave empty-handed since they were slaves and lived in bondage. You may think this story does not apply to you, but if you live a life of sin, you live in bondage. God wants to give you freedom over sin. You can live a life of freedom from bondage as you wait patiently for God to free you and bring you into your purpose.

CHAPTER 15
Persecution and Trials

After my decision to remain in the house of oppression until the Lord answered me as He promised me in prayer, I faced many trials and persecution that grew my faith. I will share a few so that your faith can grow as you see the supernatural power of God in my life and believe that He can also give you the victory over any trouble or trial you may be facing. God can heal you and give you the hope you need to see your miracles unfold.

I was prevented from attending any Christian church on Sundays and was required to do housekeeping on Sundays instead of attending church. I saw this as a way of expressing the light of the Gospel to them, so I honored them and obeyed all their requests even though they hurt me and did not give me the freedom I needed at that time. God was building my character and was teaching me to love them unconditionally as He loved them. When they saw that I was not doing any born-again activities and was not the girl they knew before boarding school, they started to search for the cause of my behavior.

I came home one night, and my aunt came into my room to talk with me. I was shocked to see her in my room, but I decided to listen to her and hear what she needed to say. She shared her heart and explained how everything changed after the family meeting that put an end to the abuse.

I tried to listen to her and pray because I had come to realize she was not my enemy. The devil was the one to blame for the pain I experienced. I loved her, and I was saddened to see her in pain even though she had hurt me. After she said what she felt, she spoke painful words that truly broke my heart. I did not respond to her because I asked God to give me the strength to keep quiet as she spoke. When she left my room, I prayed and asked God to forgive her and help me not to take offense at what she said because she did not know what she was doing. I realized she was hurt and did not know what else to give besides what she had been given.

Many people who face hurt and pain are receiving it from other broken people. You only give what you have. A broken person breaks someone else when the hurt is not revealed and healed. God is the light that shines on our brokenness and heals it. If you face any pain or were hurt by people you once trusted, you should know that there is a chance the person who hurt you was once hurt and did not heal from it. We always give what we know and have learned in childhood. It is said that hurt people will hurt others. Although the pain can be intense, we need to realize that the people who hurt us need God as much as we need Him.

When I finally got the revelation that no one in my family was the enemy and that not even the abuser was the real cause of my pain, I started to walk in my healing. I realized the relative who abused me had also been hurt, and I had to forgive him because he did not know what he had done. I also realized that my aunt said the painful words because she did not know who she was. Therefore, she did not know who I was in God. I knew that her words would not be fulfilled after I read Proverbs 26:2: "Like a fluttering sparrow or a darting swallow, an undeserved curse does not come to rest." That scripture gave me peace. I knew that everything she wished for me would not come to pass in my life because I was covered by the blood of Jesus. The Holy Spirit gave me the revelation so that I could walk in peace. I knew that no weapon formed against me would ever prosper.

A few days later, I was told that my family would not pay for my college fees. I was outraged, but I was not surprised. They changed after I told them my decision. That happened a few months before my final examinations. I knew that I was living with people who would not help me find a college or help me in any other way. I had to look for universities abroad and apply on my own. I was very determined to do all I could do and wait for God to do the impossible. The major problem was that I did not have a passport. My citizenship had not yet been approved by the government of the country I lived in.

I arrived from Uganda as a refugee after the genocide of 1994 and was only allowed to apply for citizenship at eighteen years old. I applied when I turned eighteen, but it took much longer than it was meant to take because no one was following the process. Every relative who had come was a citizen, and I was the last one to be a citizen in the country where we lived. I was praying and looking for ways to push my application to get my citizenship before I finished high school. I realized that my family was not following up with the process even though they had connections and the power to quicken the process.

I decided to follow the process on my own by going to the office that processed the application and ask them to follow up on my application. I started to battle in prayer, and I fasted believing that this mountain would fall into the sea as God promised in His Word.

When I realized that the head of the department who oversaw the application was a family friend, I understood why my application was taking so long to be approved. I decided to fight on my own. I asked for a meeting with the director of the department, which was difficult since many people knew my family. I was afraid they would find out I was following up on my application without their approval. My request to meet the director was denied three times. I was facing a wall. I did not know what else to do. I started praying and fasting, and I asked God to guide my steps and show me what to do next.

After three days of prayer and fasting, the Holy Spirit reminded me of a friend whose mother was a judge. He told me to call my friend and share my situation. My friend was very understanding and told his mother. She asked to meet with me. I was relieved that God had opened a door, and I believed He would use her to help me. She was very touched by my story and decided to help me find out why my application was taking longer than expected. I was relieved when I left her house because I knew God was moving and would create a way through her.

I started focusing on applying for universities abroad with a major in hydrogeology as I had always dreamed. I found a perfect university in Europe that offered the course I wanted, and I decided to apply. I was excited that some of my high school friends were going to study in the same area. After a few weeks of waiting for a response from the applications, I got a letter of admission from the university.

That was the best day of 2008. God moved and answered my prayers. I was admitted to my favorite college, and I could not wait to leave the house. I was so excited to share it with my closest friends and certain family members. I asked one of my closest aunts who lived abroad to help me apply for the universities.

When I got home around noon, no one was home except the housemaid who had become a good friend throughout the years. He was happy since he knew how painful it was to live in the house.

When my relatives came home, I told them that I had received a letter of admission from a university and needed to be on campus in August for the fall semester. They looked at me with straight faces and did not share my joy. I was not surprised by their reactions because they were not looking forward to me leaving the house. I was not hurt by their behavior because I was used to them. Since I had the admission letter and the help of my friend's mother to follow up with the citizenship, I was left with prayer and the hope that God would perform a miracle for me before the fall.

I woke up the following day with the determination to do my best in my studies and look for more people who could help me with my citizenship. I went back to meet my friend's mother and told her the good news. She was happy to hear I had been admitted to a university and had some news for me. She followed up with my documents and found out that my file had not been handed in. It was waiting for the court hearing with the president, and he would sign it. This was the last step for me to approve the application. Therefore, there was nothing else to do other than pray and wait for God to remind the president to request a hearing and sign the application.

I was very anxious and stressed. All that I could do was pray that the minister would hand the applications to the president before August so I could pursue my studies. I started to look for another alternative in case the citizenship was not approved before August. I wrote an email to the university and told them what I was facing. They were very understanding and extended my arrival until September.

As I pushed the dates and continued to seek help wherever I could to quicken the process, I found out that my relatives had asked to slow down the process so I wouldn't get a passport in time for my visa application. After many sleepless nights of prayer and warfare, it was August 2008, I had no citizenship and no possibility of requesting a visa. I was disappointed, and my hope was shaken. I felt as if God had forgotten me and did not see my pain. I tried to believe I would get a passport by September, but I had to decline the admission because I had no passport to leave the country.

The abuser and his friends were rejoicing that I did not get the citizenship in time. It finally arrived a few months after the college deadline had passed. My heart wanted to hate certain family members, but my spirit reminded me to focus on Jesus. I decided to pray for their salvation. The Lord reminded me to pray for my enemies and let Him fight for me.

My prayer life increased the hope and joy in my heart. I started to trust that God would move the mountain in front of me and deliver me from what I was going through. My friends were supporting me in prayer, and their parents were too.

During my nightly prayer time, a voice reassured me that God was with me and was in control of everything I was facing. I could not see it then, but today, I can testify that God was in control. He closed the door to my studies in Europe so I could grow in my faith and learn to rely on Him alone.

The following months were filled with trials and persecutions that did not destroy me. They grew me and increased my potential and my faith in God. I prayed and surrendered my studies and my pain to God. A few weeks later, I went to say goodbye to my close friends who were going to study abroad. Every day was painful. I had to say goodbye to my friends, and I did not know if my dreams would ever come to pass.

After weeks of prayer and seeking God, the Lord asked me to apply for a scholarship and a position at a public university in the city where I lived. I was not happy to hear that God's plan was for me to stay in the country and study at a public college that did not offer the major I wanted. I did not like the university and I was not happy about the word I got, but I decided to obey the Holy Spirit. I applied for a scholarship and a student position, and they were given to me a few weeks later. I was enrolled in a school I did not like and would be studying chemistry, my second least favorite major. I did not understand why God, who told me at fourteen years old that I would be a geologist, would allow to be accepted to one of the best universities in Europe and not perform a miracle to take me there. The loving God and most powerful God wanted me to study at an unstable university that had experienced many political strikes, and take a major I did not love. I could not understand how an all-sufficient God could do such a thing. It took me time to realize God was working in my heart to trust Him even when the outcome was not what I expected.

I did not know how long the wait for my freedom would take, but I decided to trust and let God do the work in me and through me. Although I was not going to study geology, I had faith that I would study geology someday and become all that God said I would be.

I put my trust in God and waited for Him to deliver me from the house of oppression. Every time I prayed, God would tell me to wait because He alone would deliver me. It took three years before I got to breathe the air of freedom and live the life I had always dreamed of living. During those three years, I had to trust Him and walk a painful path of trials and tribulations.

CHAPTER 16
Trials in School and Church

After I enrolled in first year courses of mathematics, physics, and chemistry (MPC) at the public university, with a major in chemistry, it took me a few months to start school because the university was on strike for many political reasons. We started school in 2009, and I was looking forward to studying because I did not want to stay home. I was always anxious and did not have peace at home. Our first week at school was slow because of the strike. There were about a thousand students majoring in MPC. Therefore, the auditorium for classes was sometimes too small to accommodate all the students, and people had to stand outside.

I met five friends who were from the Ivory Coast, who were very determined to excel. We all had different majors, but we decided to study together for the first year. They were all living in student dorms. No one knew my home situation because I was ashamed to tell them where I was living since my family was wealthy. They did not know the reason why I had enrolled in a public university.

Even though I did not like the classes, I focused on my studies. In my heart, I believed God could open a door to study geology. I did not know when, but I trusted that God's power would manifest in due time and He would open a door that my family could not shut.

The labor was hard, but my friend and I succeeded our first year. Even though I faced many challenges along the way, I was thankful to God for His provision. A relative gave me a gift: a plane ticket for a vacation to visit a family friend and his family. I was excited to spend time outside of the country and meet new people. When I arrived, I was welcomed by the family friend and his wife.

I later found out that his wife was born-again. We got along and spent time on the beach with her daughter and her friends while her husband was at work. One night, she and I decided to pray together. The Holy Spirit came down and reminded me of His love. I felt the hand of God wrapping me up, and a voice said, "I have not forsaken you, and you are not forgotten. Soon I will take you out of the house."

Those words strengthened my faith because I had stopped asking God to deliver me from the house a few months prior. I felt powerless and did not want to be hurt again by raising my hopes and believing that one day I would live a life free of oppression. To me, it was impossible to escape them without a passport because I was still under refugee status when the Lord spoke to me.

When I heard the tangible voice of God telling me that He did not forget me and would soon take me out of the house, I was relieved. I felt I had been forsaken, but God reminded me that it was not the case. I was thankful even though I did not know how and when it would come to pass. A part of me was at peace because I knew it was God's time to fight for me.

I went back to the room where I was staying and read my Bible. The lady came in and talked to me. She shared her story and about her walk with God. She had gone through persecution and trials after she gave her life to Jesus, but she overcame them when she stood firm in her faith. She encouraged me not to give up on my faith and trust in God. At that moment, I knew God had brought me to her place to revive my spirit and give me hope in Him. I felt as though God was speaking through her and wanted me to not give up in my faith or grow weary.

A few days later, my vacation was over and I was on my way home, filled with boldness and joy because I knew God was ready to fight for me and deliver me. At home, my aunt who was not kind to me changed and was more intentional. I was shocked to see the change of heart. I believed that God had touched her when I was away. One night she came to me and asked me if I wanted to visit a born-again church with her. One of her close friends had invited her to see her church, and she was anxious about going alone. I was surprised that she would want to visit a born-again church, but I agreed to go with her. I believed God had opened her heart to receive Him, and I was excited to see her redeemed and transformed. God started to show me His heart for her and every member of my family. I was no longer looking at them and remembering the things they did to me. I looked at them with love and prayed for them to meet the God I knew who had changed my life forever.

We went to her friend's church the following Sunday. She loved the worship and was engaged during the sermon. By the end of the service, she had decided to come back to her friend's church the next Sunday. The pastor came up to us at the end of the service and welcomed us. She was touched that the pastor greeted us, and she felt loved. She did not want to go back to the Catholic Church because she said she had encountered God and His love at that born-again church. I was excited and thankful to God for making a way in her life. I was filled with hope that her husband would also be saved.

I was allowed to go to church with my relative and was given a chance to serve at church. I was happy to serve and finally attend church on Sundays. I bonded with the church members and was hopeful about seeing a change in my family. The pastor developed a good relationship with the relative who took me to church.

After a few months in the church, we were asked to do a deliverance session and a mandatory baptism. I had not told my family that I was baptized at boarding school a few months after my salvation. Before we did the deliverance, the family member asked me not to share what had happened to me. According to her, it was a family secret, and no one should know about it. I did not argue with her, but I prayed that God would give the revelation to the minister. I went to the deliverance and prayed for God's will to be done.

On the first day of deliverance, I tried to keep the truth inside because we both did the deliverance together. However, on the last day, the Holy Spirit convicted me to be honest with the ministers, and I told them everything. They were all shocked to hear that such abomination had occurred. It seemed surreal for some of them until the relative confessed that it was true. The ministers decided to extend our deliverance so they could pray and bind all evil spirits. I was relieved after I shared my pain because I wanted to be free. I did not want to hurt any person involved, but I wanted to expose the works of the devil so God could heal me. I felt guilty for not listening to the relative, but I felt better after the session.

At the end of the deliverance session, we were baptized and welcomed as new members of the church. That was a great day of joy for us and our friends who witnessed the baptism. I resolved to worship God and surrender to Him by letting Him fight for my deliverance. A few days later, I realized that my relative who was baptized with me was still consulting witch doctors. She was making sacrifices as the other relative did every Thursday when she asked me to join a few weeks later. I had refused to do them after I accepted Jesus in my life in 2002. I knew they were deceived because they believed that witch doctors believed in God and were doing godly things. When I read the Bible for the first time in 2002, I realized how the only sacrifice God wanted from us after the coming of Jesus Christ on earth was to offer our bodies as living sacrifices to Him:

> I urge you, brothers and sisters, in view of God's mercy to
> offer your bodies as living sacrifice, holy and pleasing to
> God—this is your true and proper worship. (Romans 12:1)

When I meditated on that scripture after I was saved in 2002, I realized that Jesus was the ultimate sacrifice who saved us and redeemed our lives. As children of God, we do not need to kill an animal to redeem our sins. We are justified and made righteous for God through Jesus Christ (2 Corinthians 5:21). Therefore, when we give our lives to Jesus and become born-again, we cannot continue to practice ancestral rituals to protect us. Only the blood of Jesus Christ can protect us from evil attacks.

I was surprised to see that the relative who was baptized with me did not leave the ritual practice. She believed they were also from God. I prayed and asked God for wisdom, and He told me to be quiet and not argue with her. We continued to attend the church together, but she would sometimes go to witch doctors and ask me to keep it from the other church members. I honored her and kept her in my prayers by asking God to give her the revelation of His Word.

One morning, as I finished prayer and was ready to leave for school, she came into my room and told me I would be going to a witch doctor with another relative in two days. She did not give me a choice because she knew I never agreed with their power and always told her they were not of God. However, because I did not want to argue with her, I decided to nod and leave for my class because I was late. I decided to pray and seek guidance for what to do.

That night, I asked the Holy Spirit for guidance, and He told me to fast on the day I would go to the witch doctor. I woke up the following day and went to the witch doctor with my relative. The witch doctor lived in a small village that was three hours from our house. When we arrived, we parked next to an old house in the middle of some trees. As we stopped the car, I started praying in tongues and asking the Holy Spirit within my breath to come and hide me. The house was dark and had many bones. I was not afraid because the Holy Spirit gave me peace and assurances that He was with me and that nothing would happen. I believed God wanted to show my relative how these practices were not godly. Inside the house, an old man was sitting on the ground and writing in the sand in front of him. We were asked to enter barefoot and sit on small benches.

As we sat on the benches facing the witch doctor, the old man started talking about my relative's business and told him what would happen in his future. He gave him many details about how his business would succeed. As he spoke, I prayed in tongues softly under my breath believing that God would show my relative His power so he could believe in the true God and not the idols.

After the witch doctor spoke about my relative's business, he turned to me and started writing in the sand. He looked back at me three times with a very surprised look and was silent for a few minutes.

My relative noticed the change in posture, and he asked the old man what happened. The witch doctor turned to my relative and asked him why he had brought me to his house. He said, "Her star is hidden under the water, and I cannot not read anything about her because she is Christian. Why did you bring her here?" He got mad at my relative and said, "Take this Christian girl out of my house and never bring her back again!"

We were told to leave the witch's house immediately. That was a miracle because I had asked the Holy Spirit to be with me when I went there. The witch doctor had seen that I was Christian and could not read my life because my life was hidden in the blood of Jesus: "For you died, and your life is now hidden with Christ in God" (Colossians 3:3).

When the witch doctor said that my star was hidden in water, I automatically remembered that verse, and it gave me confidence that no evil could touch me because my life was hidden in Jesus Christ.

On our way back, my relative was very upset at the witch doctor because he did not accomplish what he intended to do. For me, the trip was one of the best testimonies of the faithfulness of God. It built my confidence because I knew that no one could harm me because my life was hidden in Christ. I started praying deeper, and my faith was strengthened after that trip.

My attention turned to serving in the church. During that time, I would go after class to serve the pastor and his family by doing whatever was necessary to facilitate the ministry. It was an honor to be part of the church family. I loved being in his house because I felt at home and never wanted to leave. I had always loved the bond between pastors and their children, and I hoped to experience it one day. I was so thankful to serve his family because he taught me many things in the ministry about deliverance, prayer, and fasting.

However, due to spiritual revelations that I received about some malicious activities done in the church, the pastor excluded me from the church. I faced my first rejection from believers, and I did not know how to recover from it. I did not understand how people of God could close their church to anyone.

My heart was broken, and I turned my heart to God, seeking His healing and revelation. As I prayed and read my Bible, I came to realize that Jesus was mostly persecuted by teachers of the law. He was even crucified by Pharisees. I came to understand that the greatest persecution would always come from believers. I had to guard my heart and not be resentful or hateful. Even though it was painful, I had to forgive them.

> *Blessed are you when people insult you, persecute you and*
> *say all kind of evil against you because of me. Rejoice and*
> *be glad, because great is your reward in heaven, for in the*
> *same way they persecuted the prophets who were before you.*
> *(Matthew 5:11-12)*

Jesus said this to His disciples before He was crucified because He knew they would be rejected and wrongly accused. In my case, I witnessed suspicious activities and was called to no longer attend the church by the leaders.

I was sad to leave the church, but I knew God had a plan for me and would fight for me. I gave my heart to God so He could heal my pain. Once again, I felt rejected. I went back to pray in my room on Sundays and read the Word of God. That brought me closer to reading more the Word of God because I did not have a pastor to teach me. I was not given permission to visit other churches, and I decided to seek God and allow Him to teach me His Word. That was a season of isolation, but it was one of the best seasons in my life. I learned to rely on the Holy Spirit for revelation, and I learned to build a great friendship with Him.

The Holy Spirit is the person who Jesus gave us when He ascended to the Father so He could give us the revelation of Jesus and the Father. Many people think the Holy Spirit is a dove or a coal of fire, but the Holy Spirit is the Third Person of the Trinity in heaven: the Father, the Son, and the Holy Spirit. He is a Person, and He is our Helper and our Counselor. He embodies many roles, but one of the most important roles is giving us the revelation of Jesus Christ.

> *But when he, the spirit of truth, comes, he will guide you*
> *into all the truth. He will not speak on his own; he will*
> *speak only what he hears, and he will tell what is yet to*

come. He will glorify me because it is from me that he will receive what he will make known to you. (John 16:13-14)

Those were the words of Jesus Christ to His disciples before He was crucified. It is important to partner with the Holy Spirit who comes in your life as you testify that Jesus is Lord (1 Corinthians 12:3).

The Holy Spirit wants to speak to us at all times and give us revelations about what is to come. I encourage you to cultivate a relationship with the Holy Spirit because He is the best friend you need. Jesus did not start His ministry until the Holy Spirit came down to the Jordan River after His baptism in the form of a dove (Matthew 3:16-17).

The Holy Spirit can take the form of a dove, but He is not a dove. He is a Person who is much alive and lives inside us. To partner with the Holy Spirit is to allow Him to guide us and speak to us. Many people have trouble listening to the Holy Spirit, but He is always speaking. We must tune in to the frequency of heaven to hear Him well. That is done in meditation on the Word of God and periods of stillness that help us listen to what He has to say. It is important to develop a listening ability so you may know what to do and where to position yourself to be in God's perfect will.

My relationship with the Holy Spirit helped me overcome the rejection I felt when I was excluded from the church. The Holy Spirit gave me peace as I leaned on Him and allowed Him to direct my steps. He also showed me how the enemy wanted to use this experience to lose my trust in the Body of Christ and never attend a church. He gave me the revelation behind the pain I experienced and gave me the strength to forgive the ministers who hurt me.

If you are saved and sanctified by the blood of Jesus Christ, the Holy Spirit resides in you and is longing to partner with you and give you the revelation of Jesus and guide you into the purpose of your life. All you need to do is listen to His voice and turn your attention to His Word. He will surely talk to you and guide you to the path of life.

CHAPTER 17
Failed Attempts

Before I was excluded from the church, I went with one of my relatives every Sunday and served joyfully. One Sunday, a special lady came and sat next to me. She was a pregnant woman who looked Rwandan and looked like someone I had met before. She sat next to me and held my hand tightly with tears on her face.

At the end of the service, she introduced herself as my father's sister. I was surprised to see her because I did not know her. I hugged her and cried with joy. She had come from Norway to see me, but my relatives did not allow it. After searching for ways to approach me, she was told I was attending the church and decided to meet me there.

When I had the family meeting in 2008, one of the family members emailed her and told her the painful news of my abuse. She was in shock and decided to come and rescue me from the house. My aunt was a very strong woman and was determined to get what she wanted. She was willing to fight, take my relatives to court, and rescue me before she left.

When we came out of the church, my aunt held me and cried. She said I looked just like my father. She had last seen me when I was four years old; before the genocide started. She asked to come with us and see where we were staying.

We all drove to the house and had lunch together. She was very kind to the other relatives. She explained why she decided to go to church. I was surprised to hear that she had tried to contact me, and no one told me. I did not know that some of my father's relatives were still alive, and

I was shocked to hear they had tried to contact me many years prior, but could not reach me.

My aunt explained why she was traveling while pregnant. She felt sad and hurt when she heard that her niece was being sexually abused by a family member. She asked my relative to let me go with her. She was ready to fight for my freedom.

After many arguments between my aunt and the relative I lived with, they agreed to let me meet my aunt the following day for one-on-one time if she agreed not to take them to court. They both agreed. I was speechless after hearing the truth from my aunt.

I got to know my aunt when I spent time with her the next day. I told her how hard it would be to take the people I lived with to court because of their connection with powerful men in politics. There was a lot of corruption in the country, and I knew she would lose because of their powerful friends. I told her how they delayed my citizenship application to stop me from leaving their house. I could not leave with her because I was still waiting for my citizenship to be approved. She realized it would be hard for me to leave on a refugee passport. Moreover, I told her not to try to take me out of the house because she could be injured and her baby could be hurt. She understood and respected my decision not to take them to court, and she flew out of the country the following day. I was sad to see her leave, but I was relieved that nothing bad had happened to her. I thanked God for protecting her.

A few months later, my father's brother tried to rescue me. Before he came, he was wise to include the people I lived with in all of his plans. Therefore, my relatives trusted him and allowed him to see me. We went to welcome him at the airport when he landed. I was excited to see him, but I could not express my excitement because I was not alone.

My uncle was excited to meet me for the first time, and he cried because he said I looked just like my father. He was a man of faith and was studying to be a Catholic priest. He could not stop crying and hugging me; just like his sister did when she first saw me. I felt a breakthrough when I met him. He told me that I was just a little girl when he last saw me.

We had dinner at home, and he could not stop crying and thanking

God for finally holding my hand. He did not want to let go of my hand. So many emotions overwhelmed him and he had no words to express them. After dinner, we spent time alone in the living room. I felt so loved by him, but I knew that I could not open up to him in the house since we were not alone. We decided to speak in our native language because I was convinced that our conversation would be taped. We talked about his family, my father, and the time he saw me in Rwanda. After an hour of talking, we drove him to the cathedral where he rented a room for visiting priests. I walked him back to his room and said good night.

When I came home, my relatives were waiting for me in the living room. One of them was holding a black folder and asked me to sit down. He looked very concerned and upset. I wondered if he had bad news. I sat down and asked myself what I could have done to make him angry. I could not think of anything I had done wrong that day or the days prior my uncle's arrival.

The relative stated that my uncle appointed people to fight against him. In his black folder were the names of the Rwandan people who had agreed to help him find a lawyer to take him to court to have me return to Rwanda with him. When I saw the folder, I knew my uncle would be in great danger if he pursued his plan to rescue me. Therefore, before the relative went on to explain what he would do to my uncle, I decided to step in and tell him that I would deny all the allegations if he promised to let my uncle go. He was shocked to hear my request and agreed to let him go if I told him that I would not help my uncle take them to court. I do not know if my decision delayed my deliverance from the house because of the fear of losing my uncle in the process. I was afraid of what my relative could do to him and answered in fear.

I could not sleep that night because I knew that I had to go the following morning to tell my uncle to forget about me and go back to Rwanda without attempting to rescue me. The only way it could work was to lie to him and tell him I was happy in the house. I was sad not to spend time with him any longer, but I wanted to spare his life so he would not die trying to rescue me. I knew what my relative was capable of doing to him and did not want him to be hurt because of me.

The following day, I woke up with a broken heart. I had to lie to my uncle and tell him I would not help him rescue me so he could be safe. I went to the cathedral and told him to go home because I was fine in the house. I gave him back his gift, as requested by my relatives, and left him there. My uncle did not understand the sudden change in my behavior and was hurt when I returned his gift to him. I asked him to leave the country immediately and told him I did not want to see him ever again, which I was required to say. On my way back, I felt broken because I had to lie to him to protect his life. My heart was aching as I left his room, but I knew that I needed to let go to spare his life.

After I came back from the cathedral, I packed my bag and left the country with the relative who abused me because he wanted to make sure I never saw my uncle again. I was hurt, but I gave my pain to God as we left the house. I traveled alone with him and was concerned that he would try to harass me, but I trusted that God would not allow him to do so.

We stayed out of the country for a few days until my uncle dropped his rescue attempt and flew back to Rwanda. We came back to a cold and tense place. God protected me on the trip and did not allow him to attempt anything.

Although my aunt and uncle were not able to rescue me from the house of oppression, I am forever grateful to them for courageously risking their lives for me. I was fortunate to meet them after I was freed from the house, and I built a strong relationship with both of them. They are my foremost cheerleaders today and they always pray for my happiness. They supported me in writing this book and always try their best to give me the love and support I need. I feel safe knowing I have them with me in this life.

God did not forget me. I was hurt by some family members, but He showed me that other relatives would fight for my well-being and do everything they could to see me whole. God is a restorer, and I see it every day as I grow closer to my aunt and uncle who risked their lives to see me free from bondage. When I was fortunate enough to see them again, I learned how to grow a healthy relationship with them. I explained my reactions when they tried to rescue me. I am grateful for their love and support. I love them dearly and know that my healing and freedom was possible because they showed me unconditional love and fought for my freedom even after they left the country.

CHAPTER 18
Trials and Tribulation

After I was excluded from the church, I spent time in prayer and reading the Word of God on my own. I noticed that the more I was digging into God's Word, the more I would face tribulation and rejection at school, at home, and in my relationships.

The first trial started one morning around three o'clock. I woke up to spend time with God in prayer, and I was praying in the spirit (spiritual tongues). I did not realize that one of my relatives was standing outside my room. Suddenly, he called my name with a loud voice. He called me out of my room and was very angry that I was praying out loud without asking for permission. He was against born-again prayers. My faith was all I had, and I could not obey their warning to not pray at home. I was ready to fight for God at any cost. After many painful words and warnings, he allowed me to go back to bed. I did not stop praying, but I became more aware of my surroundings.

One of my best friends came back for the holidays and asked me to share my testimony with her parents. They later became my spiritual parents. I told them everything that had happened to me, and they prayed for me and asked me to undergo deliverance. Since I had experienced a deliverance session in the previous church that I had been excluded from, I was afraid of being rejected again. When I got home, I prayed and asked God what to do. He told me to trust my friend's parents and do the deliverance.

A few days later, my friend's mother took me to her pastor. He listened to me for almost an hour and had tears in his eyes as I shared my testimony. He looked at me and said, "Truly, God's hands are in your life, daughter." I did not understand what he meant by that statement, but as I write this book, I can truly see God's hands in my life. I now see that God was with me in every season of my life.

After the first appointment, the pastor asked my friend's mother to bring me to church on Thursday for the midweek service. He wanted to introduce me to the lady who would do my deliverance. When we left the pastor's house, I felt so much peace and joy. I knew a new chapter was about to unfold in my life. I did not know what would happen, but I knew that I was no longer alone. God brought people who would help me break out of the bondage I was in.

The following Thursday, after school, I went to church and met the lady who was going to pray for my deliverance. I felt very connected to the lady upon meeting her. I was amazed by her love for people and her love for God. She was very gifted and always gave glory to God for all her works. After a few weeks, I knew she was the perfect person to pray for me and intercede for my deliverance. I wanted to learn from her and know more about God. We bonded, and she started to teach me about her walk with God and how to live a life that pleases God.

My first deliverance was very intense and very tiring because many spirits from generational curses came out of my body and made me weak. After my first deliverance, I started to grow more in my love for Christ. I encountered Him on a new level as I experienced His power. I learned how to consecrate my room to God so that no evil spirit could ever inhabit it.

One night I fell asleep after praying and saw a shadow at the door. My eyes could barely see who it was, but I guessed due to the size of the shadow that it was the relative who abused me. However, this time, he could not enter my room because I had anointed it. I realized how powerful the presence of God was in distancing him from me.

Many trials followed my deliverance. In fact, a little after my first deliverance, one member of my old church asked to meet me and told me horrible things that a church member said and how, after excluding me from the church, the pastor changed his sermon to emphasize more on demons and false prophets. While listening to this person, I knew that the enemy wanted me to doubt myself and think I was a false prophet.

The Holy Spirit gave me Mark 3:20-30, which states that the teachers of the law slandered Jesus and said that Jesus was possessed by Beelzebub (Mark 3:22). I realized I could not serve Christ without facing rejection from people. This incident was very painful, but it made me realize that in my walk with Christ, I would face rejection, exclusion from churches, and slander. I knew God would prepare me and give me the strength to overcome rejection and many more trials. I went back to digging deeper into God's Word and praying by relying on Him and trusting Him to mold me and train me as His servant.

One Thursday night, after school, I went to church for midweek service. I would hide going to church on Thursdays from my relatives because I was not allowed to go to church on Sundays. While I was worshipping, I felt so much heat in my hands, and the Spirit of God came down and gave me supernatural confidence and boldness in Him.

After the service, on my way home, I heard a voice saying, "You are going to eat poison that your relative made for you, but do not worry because you will not die." I was shocked, but peaceful because I believed my confidence could not be shaken. I did not know what was going to happen, but I knew that God was in control. The outcome would be in His hands.

On my way, my phone rang; it was my spiritual father. He told me that he saw the spirit of death coming toward me. He asked me not to go home. I said, "The Spirit of God told me before you called that my relative was prepared to give me poison, but nothing will happen to me. I believe God will not let me die for His namesake."

My spiritual father prayed for me, and I hung up the phone because I was receiving an incoming call. The relative who God told me about was asking how far away I was. I gently told him how far I was and hung up the phone. My flesh tried to be anxious, but I continued to praise God because I believed He would show them His mighty power.

When I got home, they were waiting for me to eat. It was not common for us to eat together. They would usually eat in the dining room together, and I would eat in the kitchen when I got home from school. I knew that what God revealed to me was about to happen. The relative told me with a smiling face that she had made my favorite soup just for me and they were eating rice and stew (African gravy). I told her that I would go put down my bag and wash my hands, and they agreed.

When I got to my room, I anointed my head and told God to have His way. While I was praying, the Holy Spirit gave me Mark 16:18:

> ". . . they will pick up snakes with their hands; and when they drink deadly poison, it will not hurt them at all; they will place their hands on the sick people, and they will get well."

This scripture strengthened me because I knew that God's Word was true, and I reflected on that scripture for several minutes.

I went into the dining room and asked if I could pray for the meal. They did not mind, which was surprising since they did not want me to pray. I prayed a simple prayer to bless the food, and after saying amen, I looked at my bowl of soup. Some black residue went up the soup and was distinctly separated from the broth. The Holy Spirit told me to eat it while praising Him in my heart and smiling at them. They ate their food and were looking at me to see if I would finish the bowl of soup. I finished it and had some more. I had no pain as I ate. The more I ate, the more confident I was that God was with me and would not allow me to die.

After dinner, I said "Good night" and went to bed. In the morning, I was awakened with a loud voice screaming, "She's still alive!" They seemed angry and frustrated that their plan had failed. I did not have any pain except a running stomach that did not last. I realized that Mark 16:18 was accomplished that night. God kept His promises again and spared my life.

A few weeks later, I came home from school at noon, and one of the relatives was at home. We had lunch together, and he told me that one of his witch doctors was coming to stay in the house for a few days and wanted to stay in my room. I was very surprised because we had two vacant rooms that could be used for guests. I did not understand why the witch doctor wanted to stay in my room. I agreed because he was ordering me to prepare my room and move out because he had already made up his mind. I was at peace because I knew my room would be ready to host the witch doctor. I planned to clean my room the next day and anoint every corner of the room, along with my clothes, so that my room would be consecrated to God and purified as the temple of God was sanctified: "Take the anointing oil and anoint the tabernacle and everything in it; consecrate it and all its furnishings, and it will be holy" (Exodus 40:9).

My room was a temple of God and my secret place with Him. I used this scripture to anoint my room and consecrate everything in it. I asked Jesus to cover my room with His blood and let His angels guard my secret place. That night, I saw three angels guarding my room. Since I knew that light and darkness cannot coexist, I believed that the light of Christ would overcome the darkness that person would try to bring to my room. I stood on the verse in John1:5: "The light shines in the darkness, and the darkness has not overcome it." I had the peace to let the witch doctor sleep in my room. I knew he could not do anything because his power would be nullified at the door.

The next day, I went to school in peace. I was confident that the three angels I saw the night before would keep my room sanctified for God. The relatives came home with the witch doctor at seven o'clock. I greeted him, and they went inside the house. I sat on the patio praying and waiting to see what God would do. Immediately, they came outside and left the house. The witch doctor said he could not stay in the house and asked them to take him to the nearest hotel because he could not invoke his gods there.

They went to find a hotel, and he never returned. I went back to my bedroom to see if the three angels were still there, and they were. I was filled with joy because God had won the battle again. My faith continued to build from one miracle after another, and I started to realize how powerful the name of Jesus was and how the darkness could not overcome Him.

After that incident, I continued to attend my church in secret. I would wake up at odd hours of the night to pray. My faith in God grew, and I decided to pray over my room and the entire house. In fact, one of my relatives used to do rituals every Thursday. When that would take place, I could feel darkness around the house. I did not know how to prevent it from overpowering the house.

One night, as I was praying before bed, I heard the voice of the Holy Spirit saying, "Pray and anoint the entire house and all the rooms." I knew that God wanted my faith to move to another level. I believed God would protect me because of all the victories I witnessed. After much thought, I found the perfect day to anoint the entire house. I decided to take a day off from my classes to clean the entire house and anoint it.

As I cleaned each room, I anointed everything in sight, including doors, beds, bathrooms, windows, walls, dressers, and clothes. Upon entering my relative's room for cleaning, I found a wooden stick with a thread underneath his pillow. In his closet, a big clay pot was filled with a dark liquid that had a very bad smell. Although it looked frightening, I felt peace in my heart. I proceeded to anoint the pot and stick because I knew God could overcome the darkness in the room.

That night, my relative came home to a clean house, which made her very happy and proud of me. She went into her room and rested. As she went to rest, I continued to pray. I asked God to encounter her as she slept. I knew the other relative would feel the change when he entered the room because the items in the bedroom were all anointed and would not work.

When I heard the other relative's car in the garage, I prayed and asked God to have His way. He walked directly to his bedroom. As he entered the room, he asked the one who was resting where I was. She told him I was in the washroom and would be out shortly. I went to the washroom to pray as soon as I heard his car because I knew he would feel the difference when he entered the house. When I heard him calling me, I was afraid, but I quickly came to myself in prayer. I asked God's presence to go with me. I prayed in tongues for a few minutes and felt the courage to meet them.

I went to their bedroom, and they were talking. I greeted the one calling me and asked him the reason for his call. He looked at me and asked where I had been. I told him I was in the washroom and hoped that he had a great day. He looked at me and did not say another word. I left their room and went to my room. I was amazed that I had God's strength to face him and talk without fear.

After a few minutes, the relative who consulted the witch doctors came out of his room. He was dressed to go out. I was amazed because we were waiting to eat with him, but he changed his mind and went out. When he left, I decided to wait for him in intensive prayer. I sensed that the enemy wanted to isolate him from the house.

I waited until 2 o'clock and went to bed. I was awakened at 4 o'clock when he returned. In the morning, I woke up and prayed for my relatives before I went out. It was a beautiful day, and I was excited to see all the great victories God had in store for us. I got ready and was about to leave when I heard my relatives talking and arguing in their room. I realized that I needed to intercede for them. I did not know the cause of their misunderstanding. The arguments became more common as I anointed the house every week.

Although I anointed the house regularly, my relatives did not stop their Thursday ritual, which led me to a new strategy. I decided to always anoint the house before and after their rituals. I was no longer afraid of anointing the places where the rituals took place. In Africa, it is very common for people to do rituals and attend churches. Witchcraft is very common, and many people consult witch doctors. My relatives would practice the rituals and also attend church often. Their practice gave me more strength to pray for them and anoint the house regularly.

One day, one of his witch doctors called the relative who practiced the rituals in the house. I was listening to him as I hid in my room. I would always hide in my room while he did his ritual before anointing the area where it was done without his knowledge. When he answered, he started to complain to the witch doctor that his business was no longer prosperous and neither were his clients. He told him how he had done all he was asked to do, but his situation worsened.

I listened to the conversation and was happy that my prayers were canceling his rituals, but I was also sad to hear that my relative's business was declining. I prayed that God would show him the right way to be successful. I decided to pray for his business and asked God to cancel all ungodly rituals in the house. The call to the witch doctor showed me how the light of God overcame darkness. When I heard their conversation, the Holy Spirit asked me to pray for the witch doctor and my relatives. They needed His light and were also His children. They needed to encounter Him. As I heard this, I was touched by the love of Jesus. I was reminded to pray for everyone; even those who work against us.

As I meditated on His Word, the Holy Spirit gave to me Matthew 5:43-48, which speaks about loving your enemies and praying for those who persecute you. Although my relatives hurt me, I was called to love them and pray for them. That was a very hard thing to do, especially when they were constantly hurting me. However, the love of God and His grace always reminded me that Jesus died for all of us. I was once lost, but now I was found by Him. I had to rise above my emotions and trust that God would fight my battles as I obeyed Him. I was called to love and honor them even when I knew they were planning to hurt me.

As you read this, you may be going through persecution and trials with loved ones without understanding why. God wants you to know that He will take you through it, and He wants you to pray for and love those who persecute you.

It can be hard to love those who hurt us and those who do not want the best for us, but God wants us to love everyone, especially our enemies. Jesus knew that His disciple Judas would betray Him, but He washed his feet along with the other disciples at the Last Supper. That was to show us that we should provide the same services for our enemies as we do for those who love us.

God is love, and we cannot hate people and claim to know Him.

> *Dear friends, let us love one another, for love comes from God. Everyone who loves has been born of God and knows God. Whoever does not love, does not know God, because God is love. (1 John 4:7-8)*

God will give you the strength to love your enemies and pray for those who hurt you because they are not the true enemies to hate. The

Bible says that our fight is not against flesh and blood, but against principalities and powers (Ephesians 6:12). The devil and his agents are our true enemies, which is why we pray for people who hurt us. God can meet them and change their hearts. It is important to know that the people who hurt us need healing just as we seek healing. Therefore, we should always lift the people who hurt us in prayer so that God can deliver them and give them a revelation of His love.

Though the trials and persecutions were many, God had a plan for me. It unfolded a few months after I anointed the house.

CHAPTER 19
The Renaissance

After three years of waiting for God's deliverance, the time finally came. In September 2010, my citizenship was approved. I was able to apply for a passport, which was processed in October 2010. As I held the passport in my hands, I knew that God's plan was about to unfold. I hid my passport at my friend's house because I was afraid my relatives would take it away.

My focus was on finding a college outside of the country where I could be admitted. Unfortunately, all college applications required money I did not have. I turned to God because I had no one to turn to for financial help. While praying, the Holy Spirit asked me not to apply to any college abroad. I was surprised, but I decided to obey. I prayed and waited for a sign from God on how to proceed.

In January 2011, God asked me to request a second deliverance at church for seven days. I doubted what I heard, but I decided to obey and proceeded to do the seven day deliverance. A few weeks after I heard about the seven day deliverance from the Holy Spirit, my relatives went out of town. That was the perfect time for my second deliverance because I did not have to worry about explaining where I was going.

The deliverance started in the second week of March 2011 and it was one of my most challenging times. Many chains were broken. On the second day of the deliverance, a specific event occurred. While the leaders were praying for me, a ring I wore on my left hand, which had been given to me by the relative who abused me, fell off my hand. I felt fire from my feet to my hands. The leaders encouraged me to throw it away, which I did it right away. As a result, the fire in my hands and feet subsided immensely.

On the third day of the deliverance, before I left the church to go home, the pastor in charge of the deliverance came to me and told me that I should be on my guard because I might have an evil attack that night.

When I went home, I was exhausted. I was physically weak because of the praying and fasting. That night, around 3 o'clock, just as the pastor had told me, I had a vivid nightmare that felt real. A short old man with a black hoodie came into my room and tried to strangle me. I pushed him to the floor and took out my sword to kill him. When I did this, he was paralyzed. I took off his hoodie, and to my surprise, his face looked like one of my family members. After taking his hoodie off, I killed him in the dream and woke up.

That was one the most terrifying dreams I ever had. I woke up drenched in sweat and physically exhausted. I prayed and asked God to give me a revelation about the dream, and the Holy Spirit gave me Ephesians 6:10-20, emphasizing verse 17: "Take the helmet of salvation and the sword of the Spirit, which is the Word of God."

I understood why I was strong enough to fight the man and why I had a sword in my right hand. I prayed for a revelation about why the man was familiar and why he tried to strangle me. The Holy Spirit told me that the strong man represented the stronghold of generational curses. He explained that I cut off the head of the man in my dream because the stronghold had no more power over my life. God destroyed the stronghold that held me in bondage for many years. I felt a sense of relief, and I felt free from the generational curses that held me in bondage.

On the fourth day of the deliverance, I woke up and felt confident that God was breaking the chains that were holding me hostage. That day was a lot deeper, and it was aligned with the six years of pain, of abuse, rejection, and trials. God was healing me in layers.

After the session, I felt lighter than ever. I knew God had healed a part of me that I thought could not be healed. I forgave all the people who had hurt me, which released me from all the prisons of offense that I had created in my heart after the abuse.

On the seventh day of the deliverance, we ended with a prayer of thanksgiving. I thanked God for healing me, breaking the chains, and setting me free from all bondage. I felt entirely renewed and freed from the burdens I carried. A prophet who was a family friend called me and said that he had a vision that many chains were breaking off of me. He did not know of my seven day session. That was a confirmation of my complete deliverance. I was confident that God had broken all the chains of bondage and would soon make a way for my breakthrough.

After the deliverance, I decided to start thanking God for delivering me from the house. I started preparing myself for the day of breakthrough. Although I did not know the exact date of my deliverance, I knew God was working and I would be delivered from the house soon. I stopped asking God to make a way and I started to give Him thanksgiving (Philippians 4:6). My heart was at peace and I lived every day as a day of deliverance.

On July 2, 2011, I woke up and felt the joy and peace of God. I prayed and dedicated my day to the Lord. After my morning activities, I decided to visit a friend that afternoon. While I was at my friend's house, I received a text message from one of my relatives who asked me to come home quickly. I was not alarmed because I was ready to leave the house and thought it was my day. After talking to my relative, I spent more time with my friend and left her house an hour later. On my way out, I got another text asking me to come home quickly because they wanted to talk to me. I started wondering about the reason for the meeting, and fear tried to invade my heart. I did not let fear overcome me because I trusted God to have His way. I prayed and asked my spiritual father to keep me in prayer as I went home.

A week before, I had called my aunts who lived abroad and told them of my intention to leave the house because I had received my passport and could leave the country. I told them because I needed the help of my family abroad to leave the country. They agreed with my decision and offered to help me in any capacity. Therefore, on July 2nd, when I received the call from my relative at my friend's house, I was ready to leave the house if asked.

At home, my relatives were waiting in the living room with my journals in front of them. They had found out about the anointing of the house, my church attendance, the deliverance, and the words of the Holy Spirit contained therein. After sharing many painful words, they announced that I was no longer allowed to pray in my room, read the Bible, or attend church services.

It was my turn to speak. I felt violated by them reading my journals and going through my personal belongings without my permission. I was no longer ready to agree to their instructions. These decisions were out of line and would require me to be bound again. Since they had read my journal, they knew all about my encounters and what I did after hearing the voice of the Holy Spirit to be delivered.

I told them with a bold voice that I could not follow their instructions because God was everything I had. I told them how I could not live without praying to God. Prayer was the one thing that sustained me and gave me hope for my future. I chose God over their instructions, and I would never stop praying or praising Him because He had changed my life.

As I was sharing my thoughts, they were quiet. They did not reply to what I said and dismissed the meeting. At the end of the meeting, I felt like my breakthrough had arrived. I knew God had already started to work within me. I went to my room feeling peaceful and surprised by my response. I had never faced them and talked to them in that way. I did not cry in front of them or in my room when I was alone. I got ready for bed and prayed. I asked God to come and tell me the next step to take in the next days to come. Around five o'clock, I was awakened by someone's hand on my face. It was the relative who abused me. I was very frightened and did not know why he was in my room. I pushed him away and asked him to leave my room with a straight voice. I was angry about seeing him in my room without permission.

When he left the room, I cried out to God and asked Him what to do. I was too tired to fight him again. As I cried out to God, I heard the Holy Spirit saying, "Today is the day of your freedom, Aline! Wake up, take a shower, and wait for My direction to leave the house. I do not want you to take anything as you leave except your Bible. You will walk out of this house and never come back again."

I was filled with peace and did exactly as I was told. I waited for the Holy Spirit's signal to leave. I cleaned my room and put out all the important documents they would need when they found out I was not coming back. I tried to leave a letter to explain my decision to leave, but the Holy Spirit did not let me do so.

At eight o'clock, I left my room and walked toward the gate. My aunt was taking care of her garden. She asked me where I was going since it was Sunday, and I replied that I was going for a walk. I did not add another word. I looked at her like it was the last time because I believed that I might not see her again. I felt a bit sad, but I was at peace because I knew God was delivering me and answering my prayers.

I called my spiritual father to let him know that I had left the house. He sent someone to pick me up and take me to church.

When I entered the church, they were all waiting for me. I felt peace because God had freed me from the house of oppression. I worshipped God for the first time without fearing that anyone would see me and report me to my relatives. I was not in a hurry to go to a house that brought sadness to my heart. I had glimpsed freedom and was excited for my new journey.

Although I did not know what would happen next, I was at peace. I knew God would hide me and not send me back. I called my aunts before I decided to switch off my cell phone. I wanted them to know I had finally left the house. They were very surprised and worried. They did not know where I was or what my next plan would be. I knew that I was out of the house and the next step would be given as I trusted God.

At the end of the church service, we drove to my friend's house to decide what to do next. We all knew that my relatives would not let me go easily. They would look for me everywhere. After many discussions, my spiritual father decided that the church would be the best place to hide me since my relatives knew them and their house. We drove back to the church at six o'clock. The pastor of the church was waiting for us and prayed with us. He showed me where I would be staying, and he congratulated me for deciding to leave the house.

After prayer, the pastor got a phone call from a woman in her church whose husband was in politics. She advised me to talk to a Captain at the police department who could help me figure out the next step to make my freedom permanent. The Captain was a friend of hers, who she believed to be the best person to speak to. After she gave me his contact information, I resolved to meet him the following day.

My relatives started looking for me a few hours after I left. They went to my friends' houses, including the house where I had been a few hours before. They told my friends that I was missing and asked if they had seen me the day before. God protected me and did not allow them to find me at my friend's house. They arrived after I had left the house.

On Monday, July 4th, I woke up and got ready to meet with the Captain. For my safety, I wore Muslim attire that hid my face, as I did not want people to recognize me as I went to the police department. I arrived around noon and was directed to the Captain's office. He was waiting for me and greeted me with a smile. I told him everything and explained why I had left the house and was staying at the church. I knew my relatives wanted me to go back to their house.

After a short break, the Captain looked at me and told me that he believed my story, but the only way I would be free would be to leave the country. The officer suggested looking for a visa to any other country. He would help me leave the country because my name was everywhere and it would be hard to leave without his help. However, he told me to leave town and call them from a public phone to let them know I was safe and would not come back home. The Captain asked me to contact them so they would not have any reason to pursue me. If I was not in danger or kidnapped, they couldn't ask the police to look for me.

I left the office and drove to a small town. I called my relative, and she was relieved to hear my voice. She asked where I was, but I did not tell her. I let her know that I would not come back because I had decided to leave them. She was very angry and repeated the same things she always used to tell me. I ended the call because I was told not to speak for too long; otherwise, they could trace the call and find where I was calling from. I went back to church, spent time in prayer, and waited for my friend's parents to come and pray with me.

My spiritual father and his wife came to hear about the meeting with the Captain. They prayed for me and decided to take me back to their home. They believed that my relatives would not go back to look for me at their house. I was relieved to go with them because I always felt protected in their house.

We drove back to their house, and they decided to give me a new name in case someone went to look for me. I started to pray and seek God for guidance. I wanted to seek God's face to know where to apply for a visa. I had tried to visit my aunt in Europe a few months prior to my decision to leave, but had been denied a visa. I thought it would be hard to apply for a Schengen visa. I got a phone number and contacted all my relatives who lived abroad.

The wait was done in prayer and seeking counsel from other Christians about what to do next. My relatives did not stop looking for me after I called them. In addition to sending police to search for me, they also consulted witch doctors to see where I was hiding. I could see all their tricks because the Holy Spirit revealed it to us in prayer. Their attempts failed because I was hidden in the shadow of God's wings: "Because you are my help, I sing in the shadow of your wings" (Psalm 63:7).

I realized that because God's hand was upon my life, I would not be found by them. Hence, I focused on finding an alternative way to leave the country because I knew that my freedom would only be manifested if I left the country. I did not lose hope when I could not see the answer because I trusted God's Word in Psalm 27:14 "Wait for the Lord; be strong and take heart and wait for the Lord."

Some days were harder than others. My flesh would doubt God's Word, but I always remembered His faithfulness. I knew that He would fulfill His promises in my life and make a way for me to escape. While I waited, I decided to remind myself of all the miracles God had created in my life. He continued to protect me. I lived a mile away from the house of oppression, but no one knew where I was. God showed me how He could hide me in the presence of my enemies.

CHAPTER 20
The Way Out

After I left the house of oppression, I spoke to my uncles and aunts who lived abroad and were willing to help. I did not give them the details of where I was staying because I did not want them to worry. I also did not want the information to reach the people I was hiding from.

An aunt contacted me and suggested that I should apply for a South African visa. Her brother was living there and could accommodate me. That was a brilliant idea because I did not want to apply for a Schengen visa and be denied for a second time. I did not know the uncle who lived in South Africa, but I was willing to try this alterative and leave the outcome to God. After many prayers, I decided to apply for a South African visa.

After gathering the required documents, I went to the South African embassy. I went on my own for safety. We did not want my relatives to find out where I was living or who was helping me. I was worried that I would be denied the visa, but I trusted God to make a way if it was His will. I did not speak English fluently since I lived in a French-speaking country.

When I arrived at the embassy, I waited to be called for an interview. I was stressed because I did not know what to expect from the interview. When the lady called my name, I went forth, calling the name of Jesus in my heart. The lady was frightening and made me feel uneasy. She looked at my documents and told me there was one missing document, which prevented her from accepting my application. I left the embassy and called my cousin who was helping her father by sending the documents.

Two days later, I went back to the embassy with all the required documents. The lady who took my documents the previous time was not working. The new lady seemed more genuine than the previous one. She took my application and told me they would contact me when they were done reviewing my application. I went home, thanked God, and asked for His favor upon my application. I knew God would open the door to South Africa if it was His will. The Holy Spirit gave me peace about the outcome. I was confident that a door would open. The Holy Spirit had asked me to only apply for a South African visa, and I did as He had told me to do.

A few days went by with no calls from the embassy. My spiritual father assured me that it sometimes took two weeks to receive their call. I tried not to be anxious and spent my days in prayer. I was seeking God's peace and guidance for the next step to take. As I waited for the call, I drew closer to God. I realized that worrying would not quicken God, but peace and trust in God would drive out the enemy. I started to spend more time with God, and I went to other deliverance sessions at my church. The more I was in God's presence, the more I could feel His touch and assurance that He was in control.

Many events and trials happened as I stayed with my spiritual parents. My relative tried to attack me with his witch doctors, but prayer and the name of Jesus always overcame the enemy's trials. I started to see the power of the name of Jesus. I saw how the enemy always tried to take me back into the darkness.

I experienced the presence of God and His unconditional love toward me. As I was seeking His face, I came to realize that I needed to forgive my relatives and repent on their behalf for all the idolatry that was done when I was living with them. I realized the enemy was the one to hate and not them. They were just the instruments of His works. This revelation came after reading a few scriptures in the Bible, including Ephesians 6:12 and 1 John 4:8. Through prayers and wise counsel, I learned to let go of my anger and trust that God would start the healing process and set me free from my fears and pain.

Although I had left the house of oppression, I was still filled with the fear of being caught and taken back to them. While waiting for the embassy to call, I went through a series of events that made me believe that my relatives would not allow me to leave the country. In my nightmares, I was taken back to the house and my conditions became worse. I wondered what they would do to me if I went back to their house. I had no choice, but to wait for the embassy to call with a pleasing answer.

One night, I could not sleep and rehearsed past events that left me overwhelmed with emotions. After praying and pouring my heart out to God, I realized the pain was not my burden to carry. I had to give it to God so He could heal me. I was reminded that God allowed me to leave the house and protected me through it all. He was faithful to seeing me through this. I went to the bathroom because I did not want to wake up the people who were in my room, and I cried out to God.

It was no longer a cry of desperation. It was a sign of complete surrender to the outcome. God had a plan, and His ways would be far better than mine. I was ready to stay in the country for as long as He needed me to stay there. After surrendering to Christ, I felt the weight lift from me. The peace of God came to my heart and I could feel His tangible presence as I called upon the name of Jesus. I did not want to leave His presence.

I fully understood what David said in Psalms 84:10 regarding a day in the court of the Lord being better than a thousand elsewhere. I felt forever safe in His arms, and I knew that nothing would happen to me because He was covering me in His arms. Even though I had no other plan besides the South African visa, I was assured that God had a plan. I chose to trust Him.

After the night of surrender, I woke up as a new person. I was no longer afraid of being caught by my relatives. I decided to start packing in faith that God would do the impossible. After ten days of waiting, my spiritual father suggested that I ask for a follow up at the embassy since it was my right to do so. I went to the embassy the following day, which was the day before my scheduled date of departure.

As I arrived at the entrance to the embassy, my heart was beating at an unusual pace because I was about to discover if my visa application was approved or not. I did not know what to request and decided to pray before entering. As I prayed, the peace of God filled my heart. I knew He was in control. I sat down and waited for my name to be called.

Two men arrived before me and were waiting with me. One of them was immediately denied the visa and was very upset. As the second man went forth, I saw that the lady I had first met was working. She did not seem genuine to the man who was denied the visa. I did not let the situation frighten me. I prayed and felt the peace of God and His joy in my heart, which reminded me that God was in control and not the lady in front of me. I sat patiently because I knew God would give me the words to say when it was my turn.

Suddenly, a very well-known man of God who was preaching on national television came in with another man. I was very excited to see him for the first time because I listened to his sermon and was blessed by his ministry. The man of God greeted me with a genuine smile and handshake before he and the man with him sat next to me. I was very impressed by his humility and desire to wait his turn even though he was given the choice of going ahead of me.

As he sat next to me, I felt in my heart that I should comment on his sermons and share how it blessed me in painful times. He was happy to hear my compliment and asked if I had a prayer request that he could pray for me. I was shocked that a man of God of his influence would ask me for a prayer request. I told him that I wanted to visit my uncle in South Africa, and my second prayer request was for God to glorify His name in my life.

He looked at me with a smile and said, "Surely our God will answer your prayers." The man of God with his friend held my hand and prayed for me.

I was very emotional during the prayer. In his prayers, he prophesied that I would be a servant of God all the days of my life, but he did not ask God to let me visit my uncle. I thanked him because he believed that God had already answered my prayer.

The prayer was not very long, but I felt the presence of God in every word he spoke. After the prayer, he hugged me and told me that he hoped to see me in South Africa because he was going to a conference in Johannesburg. After the prayer, he was called to receive his passport because he was flying to Johannesburg that night. Before he left, he looked at me with a smile and told me that God had answered my prayer. He told me to rejoice. I was happy to hear how God would use me to serve Him all the days of my life and how He had already answered my prayers. However, my human mind could not help but wait to see because I was still waiting for my name to be called before I could fully rejoice. I thanked God as the man of God asked me to do.

It was my turn to go forth and ask for a follow-up. When I faced the lady who turned down my application, I was no longer afraid of her. I boldly asked for a follow-up since my scheduled date of departure was the following day. She took my information and went to check on the reason for the delay. As she went away, my heart was shaking. I wondered what she would say when she returned. My spirit was at peace, and I remembered what the man of God had said to me before he left.

A few minutes later, she came back and told me they had investigated my case, which was the reason of the delay, and it took longer than expected. However, after their investigation, they decided to give me a thirty day visiting visa. As she was explaining, another lady called her into her office. She excused herself and left for a second time. I was happy to hear that I had been given a month visa. I was excited and could not wait to let my family know about the miracle God did for me. The thirty day visa was more than enough because I only needed a way to leave the country and I was at peace for God's outcome. I knew God would open another door if needed.

After a long wait, a tall white lady came out and called my name. She was not the same lady who had given me the information. She seemed very concerned, which made me stress as she walked toward me. She introduced herself as the diplomat in charge of signing every visa that was presented at the consulate. She asked many questions about my uncle and where I would be staying.

I answered with peace and told her that my uncle would take care of me. Even though I had never met my uncle, I saw his kindness and determination to help me. I told her how he was excited to see me for the first time and how his family could not wait to spend time with me. I also told her how my uncle said he would do anything that was needed to make my stay memorable.

She asked me when I was planning to leave, and I answered that my plane ticket was for August 27th, which was the following day. After interrogating me, she called the first lady and asked her to change the visa from thirty days to three months. They canceled the thirty day visa, which was already printed in the passport, and put in another visa. She asked me to take a seat and wait for them to change it.

I was very surprised by the change and could not contain my joy. I called my family and told them that I had the visa and was waiting to receive my passport with the new visa. The man of God was right and had prophesied that I would be given a chance to meet my uncle and would be given more time to spend with him.

While waiting for my passport, I realized it would be my last Friday in the country. I felt nostalgic and was sad to leave the people who had become family. I knew that it would be hard to go back to the country where I grew up and encountered God. I was excited to see the next chapter of my life unfold, but I was sad about leaving my childhood and past behind me.

They gave me the passport at 3:16 p.m., and I was the last client to leave the embassy. When I left the embassy, I went to the travel agency to pay for my flight ticket and called the Captain who had asked me to call him as soon as I got the visa. I told him that my flight would leave at 4:00 p.m. the following day. To my surprise, he asked me to arrive at the airport at 3:45 p.m. and wait for his call.

I went home and started packing because we had a night vigil at church. I was excited and amazed about how my day had gone after I saw a mighty man of God who prayed for me and prophesied about my life. I was fortunate to speak to the consulate diplomat in charge of the visa application, receive three times the amount of days that were initially given, and pay for my plane ticket. I could not stop thanking God for His work and miracles that overwhelmed my heart.

When my spiritual parents came home, they were very thankful for the miracles that occurred and prayed for me before they gave me more advice about how to be when I got to South Africa. I realized that my freedom would mean being physically away from them, and I had not yet made peace with that idea. I had grown close to them and they had become my parents. They showed me the unconditional love of God and taught me how to seek the presence of God.

I was finally at the door of my breakthrough, but I could not fully rejoice because I had to say goodbye to the people who loved me the most and had been used by God to hide me when I left the house of oppression. Although God had answered our prayers, the thought of leaving them behind was hurting me. I did not know when I would see them again.

After packing and praying, we went to church. I met with my pastor and told him the good news about the embassy and how I was leaving in a few hours after the night vigil, which ended at six o'clock. He prayed and gave me his blessings for the next chapter of my life. The pastor encouraged me to trust God about my future because He would surely go ahead of me and make a way. As he blessed me and spoke about my bright future, my heart ached. I did not know if I would ever see him again or if I would ever go back to the church where God delivered me and gave me the peace to withstand the unknown.

On my way home after the night vigil, a large flock of birds came toward me as I was driving. I shouted, "Jesus," and they all scattered. I was amazed by how powerful the name of Jesus was and how God protected me from an accident. I was thankful and went to bed as soon as I got home. I woke up at ten o'clock and finished packing.

After packing and spending time with my friends, I had to start saying goodbye to people individually. The woman of God who did my deliverance came to say goodbye and prayed for me as I was standing in my breakthrough. I had grown close to her after I left the house. She taught me how to speak and declare in faith the promises of God. Her walk with Christ always challenged me to surrender everything to God. Her life and devotion to Jesus always gave me the hope to serve God and seek Him better.

She requested time to talk with me alone. I was sad to say goodbye to her because she had become an aunt to me and taught me many things in my walk with God. She started telling me how grateful she was that God had made a way for my freedom. She prayed for me and gave me advice about what to do when I got to South Africa.

After my talk with the woman of God, I was called by my girlfriend whose house I was staying in. She came home with my other three close friends and was waiting for me in the living room. I wiped my tears after talking to the lady who had become a close aunt and went to meet them in the living room. When I saw my friends, I was reminded of the day I finally shared my pain, and they prayed me back to God. They were the reason for my breakthrough. God allowed me to tell them the truth, and they asked their parents to help me.

Those four girls had become my sisters, and I knew that I could count on them wherever God would take me. They contributed to my freedom with their love and support as well as the support and prayers of their families. I had many people standing with me and praying for my freedom.

When they saw me coming into the living room with my aunt, they rushed and gave me a group hug with joy. They were witnessing my freedom. As I hugged each girl, I was reminded that I would say goodbye to them without knowing when I would see them again. Although I was excited to start a new life, I was sad to leave my friends and loved ones behind. I had become close to their families, and it was hard for me to say goodbye. My eyes were filled with tears of joy and beautiful memories as I hugged them. I thanked them for supporting me and praying for me when I could not do so. I also shared how grateful I was to God for bringing them into my life. We all prayed for one another and promised to follow God no matter where He took us. After spending a few moments with them, they helped me finish packing and we waited for my spiritual parents to arrive for corporate prayer and words of advice.

At three o'clock, we all prayed as a family and headed to the airport. I was somewhat worried that the people my relatives asked to find me would see me as I embarked and try to stop me. In fact, my relatives gave my name and picture to the airport police so I could not leave the country. However, before I could let the worry take my mind, the

Holy Spirit assured me that He was in control and would not put me to shame.

As we arrived at the airport, we waited for the exact time given by the Captain before calling him. When the time came, I called him and he told me to wait for two officers who would escort me to the plane. I said goodbye to my friends and my spiritual parents who had become dear to my heart and received their blessings.

Two officers walked me to a plane that was about to take off. A part of me could not believe that I could leave the country and would not be stopped. When we got to the plane, the officers escorted me to my seat, took the information from my passport, and left. As I sat on the plane and gave the officers my details, I was afraid it would turn into a nightmare where the plane would be stopped and my relatives would come and take me back to their house.

Five minutes after I sat down, the plane started moving. I started to believe I was finally leaving the land of my sorrow and going into a new land of joy and healing. I could not stop praising God for His miraculous hands and power over my life. I had a layover in Accra, Ghana, and I changed planes. That country reminded me of many vacations, which hurt, but it was used by God as a place of transition to change my memories from pain to strength and miracles. I never thought Ghana as a country of painful memories after my layover. It was a place of transition from bondage to freedom. God wanted to redeem my memories of Ghana and chose to make me stop there on my way to my freedom so I would remember it as a stop on my walk to victory.

Although I left the country of fear and bondage, I was still afraid that my relatives would find me in Ghana when we stopped and changed planes. I remembered the way I felt when we landed in Ghana, and it reminded me of the Book of Exodus when the Israelites left Egypt and were walking. They thought Pharaoh would find them and take them back to slavery, but Pharaoh did not take them back to Egypt even when he found them and sent his chariots to get them back. God parted the Red Sea for them and allowed the Israelites to walk on dry ground in the Red Sea. The Egyptians drowned and did not reach the Israelites.

I spent my layover in Ghana in prayer. I was excited to see the country that would be marked as the gateway to my freedom. My heart was relieved as we took off from Ghana. I knew nothing could stop me anymore. I saw the power of God manifested in my life when I was told that we would soon be arriving in Johannesburg. I knew my relatives could no longer take me back to the house of oppression. God assured me that He would fight my battles and make sure that no one could see me at the airport and the flight taking off for South Africa. I was astonished by God's great power and might that moved me out of the country with no apparent trouble. I asked God to give me peace and trust that He would take me to South Africa as He promised. The more I prayed and read my Bible, the more peaceful I became. God gave me the assurance that I would arrive in South Africa and would declare His wonders.

After three hours, we took a second plane that flew straight to Johannesburg South Africa. In the plane, I finally got to close my eyes. I was safe, and my freedom was won by God. When the pilot announced that we were landing in Johannesburg, I was grateful for a safe flight. The flight took eight hours, and we finally landed in Johannesburg on August 28th, at five o'clock and applauded the pilot.

It was early in the morning, but my eyes were open because I could not wait to see my cousins and my uncle. I remembered the man of God who I met at the embassy before I got my visa. He mentioned that I might see him in Johannesburg and I did not know that would be my destination. Therefore, I knew God had spoken through the well-known pastor to prophesy over my life. I was grateful for the work of God and His protection around me. My heart was full of expectations, and I could not wait to meet my uncle and his family. Although I did not speak English and was told his daughters only spoke English, I trusted that God would allow us to understand each other since they understood a little of our native language.

CHAPTER 21
A New Beginning

After collecting my luggage, I went out and saw two ladies holding a white paper with my name on it. I immediately saw that they were my cousins because I had seen a picture of them that my aunt sent before I left. I smiled and ran to them with tears in my eyes. They hugged me with joy and introduced themselves to me. I was relieved that I was finally in South Africa with my family. I was exhausted from the journey, but I was excited to get to know them.

They took my luggage and called a cab that took us to their apartment. After a few minutes in the cab, we arrived at a beautiful and peaceful apartment. I knew it would be my place of new beginnings. The oldest cousin I communicated with as I prepared for the visa application was the only familiar voice I knew. She was excited to finally meet me because she had heard so much about me. She could not wait to hear my full story because she said I was a living miracle. She was a lovely person and immediately showed me the entire apartment. It was six o'clock, and they had not slept because they were waiting for me. The second cousin was also thrilled, but she struggled to communicate with me because she did not speak our native language. We communicated with signs, which was fun because she made me feel at home immediately.

After exchanging few words, we went to bed and slept for a few hours. I arrived on a Sunday, and they had many things planned for when we woke up. I closed my eyes and slept peacefully because I was far away from my relative and he could no longer take me back to their house. That was one of the best sleeps I have had because I did not have any nightmares. I was not stressed about what was going to happen. I was resting peacefully because God had shown me His power and might by rescuing me from the country of my bondage. I felt like a born-again child, and I could finally breathe the air of freedom. I could pursue my dreams and be what I had always longed to be.

We woke up around noon and went shopping for groceries. The eldest of my cousins cooked for us, and we got to know each other. Later in the afternoon, their father came home. He lived five hours away from Johannesburg. I was excited to meet him and felt peace and safety in his presence. He told me about how happy he was to have me in South Africa and how I was no longer alone. I had a family who would fight for me and keep me safe. I felt loved and protected by family members for the first time. I knew from then on that I did not have to fight alone. I had people who would protect me and were there for me. Although there was a language barrier, I had never felt as loved and safe as I did with my family in Johannesburg.

During my first week in Johannesburg, I started focusing on what to do next for my future. However, a few days after I arrived, I had an attack that made it hard for me to walk. I had a boil that started getting bigger after hours. It would hurt at night. I knew it was an attack because the pain would increase when I prayed and called on the name of Jesus.

I called my spiritual father after going to a dermatologist with my cousin's friend. I told him what had happened. He prayed for me and asked me to anoint the boil with anointing oil. As he prayed for me, I felt the fire of God in my right hand going toward the boil. The boil started burning, and I felt immense heat from my thigh down to my feet. When I opened my eyes, the boil was gone. I was astonished and glorified the name of Jesus. I knew the enemy was not done fighting against my freedom, but I also knew prayer and my faith would take me through.

After I hung up the phone, I repented for worrying and lacking faith. When I saw the boil, I started to give in to fear instead of praying and seeking God's face. After praying and repenting, I was convinced that God would restore all that I had lost while I was in bondage.

I will repay you for the years the locusts have eaten—the
great locusts and the young locust, the other locusts and
the locust swarm—my great army that I sent among you.
(Joel 2:25)

I learned to trust God in the process of healing my heart from the trauma by sharing my story with my family and friends. I blended into the family and was welcomed as a sister and daughter. I finally learned what it meant to be loved unconditionally by your family. The more I shared my story about what I had gone through, the more peace I felt in my heart. I felt God ministering to me and healing every ache and pain. I learned about my family's history, and I learned to lean on them and look forward to a better future.

After two days with us, my uncle left Johannesburg and went back to his town. He stayed in a small town with his wife and his two youngest children. I was happy to finally belong in a family who loved me unconditionally. I looked forward to meeting the other children and getting to know them. We resolved to wait for his wife. She would take me to their town a few days later.

The night after my uncle left, I had a high fever and threw up the entire night. I felt dizzy and thought I had food poisoning, but the feeling went on the next morning. I called my cousin at work, and she sent one of her friends to take me to the hospital. When we got to the emergency room, they did some tests and concluded that I had malaria. That disease is only found in third world countries and is caused by mosquito bites. Since South Africa was not a country with malaria, they did not have the medication to cure it. Therefore, they only gave me medication to lower the fever and stop the nausea.

Malaria is deadly when it is not cured immediately. The friend who drove me to the hospital was a doctor and gave me more medication to reduce the fever while I waited for the malaria treatment. When we got home, I called my spiritual father and asked him to send the treatment immediately. The medication was not hard to find in his country since malaria was common there. With no cure, the virus would reach the bloodstream and cause irreversible damage. It can cause damage in the liver cells or the brain, which results in immediate death. For these reasons, it was always recommended to start taking the medication from the moment you saw the symptoms so the virus could be neutralized before going further in your immune system.

As planned, my aunt came to take me to her home the day after I started to be sick. She came earlier so she could take care of me. My cousins were not home because of their work and my aunt wanted me to be alone while I was sick. She took me to her home so she could take care of me. I left my cousins' apartment and missed them because they had become my sisters. They were a great support to me and I was grateful to have them.

My aunt and I took the bus to her town. I was very sick and did not enjoy the journey. The motion made me sicker. When we arrived, my aunt took me to my room and cooked for me. She was the best mother I had ever had, and she made me feel better with her love and hospitality. They became my parents and I was amazed to see their love and concern for me.

At night, the fever went up. As my situation worsened, my uncle gave me some medication to reduce the fever. He resolved to take me to the hospital the following day. I could barely walk, and I started to lose any hope of being healed. The medication was taking longer than I thought it would, and I knew it would be hard to heal after having malaria in my bloodstream for days. I cried out to God because I was out of remedies. I asked my aunt to call my pastor so he could pray for me one last time. I was convinced it was my last chance to say goodbye. He prayed for me, assured me that God would heal me, and told me I would glorify God's name. I listened to him, and my hope increased as he prayed for me. I remembered God's miracles, and I knew He could heal me again. I believed God would give me a miracle as we drove to the hospital.

My uncle and his wife took me to a hospital that had just been built. The hospital started operating two weeks prior to the day we went there. My uncle was convinced that they would have the medication for malaria since the town had people from Namibia and Zambia where malaria was common.

As we entered in the hospital, my uncle met a doctor he knew and felt reassured that he could help me. He told him how it had been five days without medication since I was diagnosed with malaria in Johannesburg.

The man looked at me as he was about to leave and said, "There is nothing we can do to heal her. Just take her home."

My uncle was furious and did not let the doctor finish. He walked away and took me with him. He went inside and asked other doctors to help him since his daughter was in critical condition. After a few minutes, there was a breakthrough. The doctor who was on call that day was Nigerian and had the medication for malaria. This was a miracle of God to meet a doctor with the treatment. I was hospitalized and immediately given the prescription with drips because I could not keep anything in my stomach. I was put to sleep, and I woke up when the nurse came to change the drip. My aunt was sitting next to the bed and told me what had happened. I realized that God had started the process of healing in my body and in my heart. I was thankful that God had allowed my uncle not to be stopped by the man who had told him to give up. He chose to go forth and ask other doctors for help. She told me about how the Nigerian doctor was the only one who had the medication, and happened to be on call when we arrived. After a few hours with my parents, they were asked to leave because they could not sleep at the hospital.

When they left, I went into a deep sleep and had dreams about my future. God started to minister to me. He told me what I was going to do and how the next years were going to unfold in my life. I knew nothing could stop my purpose because my life was hidden in Him. I know you may say that I could not lose hope after all He took me through because He showed His power repeatedly. However, this disease made me wonder if I would survive, especially when I heard the doctor telling my uncle to take me home because the only thing to do was wait for my death. It magnified my fears and I forgot where God took me from and how He protected me from poison, accidents, and death.

For me, it took many seasons of trials to realize that God was always in control and was taking care of me at all times. I came to realize that no matter what I faced God was with me and would always take me through things.

As I am writing this, I would like to take a moment to encourage you to look for the wonderful things God did for you when you faced the darkest seasons of your life. The enemy wants us to focus on what we go through and forget what God did before. He took us out of painful situations (disease, broken relationships, etc.), and God can do the same thing again if we trust Him. The only thing that stays constant in our lives is the consistency of God. Jesus never changes. He is the same yesterday, today, and forever. Therefore, we can rest assured that if God moved mountains before, He is also capable of doing it today even though it might not be the same outcome we expected. God is unlimited and faithful.

When Jesus enters our lives, He not only takes the perfect parts we want Him to have, but He embraces the parts we try to hide, all of our imperfections, brokenness, and limitations. He loves us unconditionally and there is nothing we can do to deserve His love, or run away from His love. No matter what comes your way to make you doubt His love, know that Jesus cannot leave you because His love is unfailing and never leaves you alone (2 Timothy 2:13; Romans 8:38-39).

I did not realize how faithful God was until I looked back as I wrote this book. I realized that I was not forsaken or forgotten for a moment. I found out that it was good for me to go through all of my pain so I could relate to other people who had similar pain. God's love is unfailing and His mercy is renewed every morning. I understood that God did not allow the abuse or the death of my biological parents to destroy me because He had a bigger plan that only He knew. In fact, God turned what the enemy had meant for evil into the great testimony I am sharing with you today.

In the hospital, I encountered God when a voice spoke to me and said that I would not die and would declare the wonders of God. The voice told me that my life would be a living testimony of God's faithfulness and would bring many men and women out of bondage. As I heard His voice, I recognized it. It was the same voice that met me when I was in boarding school and told me about my first assignment. I knew then that my life was no longer meant to be lived on my own. I welcomed God into my life again and asked Him to guide me and use my life to glorify Him. As I prayed, I saw a bright light filling my hospital room. Joy filled my soul. I knew God had answered my prayers, and from that moment on, I felt better. My strength came back, and I was released from the hospital two days later.

Before they released me, they checked my organs for damage since it had taken a few days before treating the virus. The doctor was surprised at the test results because it looked like my blood cells and organs had not been damaged. They said I was lucky because it was not common for someone who suffered malaria and reached the level I was when I was hospitalized, to be alive. I knew it was not pure luck; it was God's healing and faithfulness in my life. As the doctors left my room, I thanked God. My confidence and strength came back.

I was discharged from the hospital and went home with parents who were grateful to witness my healing. I have called my uncle and his wife my "parents" from the time I got to know them because their love for me healed the wounds of my childhood.

I recovered and started planning for my future. As I prayed, the Holy Spirit told me I would not stay long with my parents. I would go back to Johannesburg and start studying English because I was a French speaker. After a month, I went back to Johannesburg as the Lord said. The Holy Spirit told me to look for institutions that taught English to foreign students. This was the first step because every university required a certificate of English efficiency for every foreign student. My ultimate goal was to be enrolled in a college and study what I always wanted.

I did not know the city of Johannesburg, and I did not want to apply to an institution that God did not approve of. I started a program of prayer and fasting for three days and waited for direction about where to apply. On the second day of the fast, the Lord told me the name of the university where I would study geology and the name of the institution where I would study English. I was surprised by the name of the university since it was not located in Johannesburg. It was in

Pretoria which is the administrative capital of South Africa. I had no family members in Pretoria to stay with. I started to think about how I would live and study, but the Holy Spirit stopped me. He told me He was in control and had already saved my place and no one would take it from me. I was relieved that God was in control and did not ask any more questions.

To study at the university, the Holy Spirit told me I had to get a student visa. I had a visitor's visa that did not allow me to apply without changing it. I had to think about how to change the visa type without returning to the country I came from. After many prayers and advice from family members, we concluded that I needed to apply for a Rwandan passport. That was the only way I would not have to go back to the country of my bondage. After receiving the Rwandan passport, my plan was to apply for a student visa in South Africa or go to Rwanda and apply from there. I had not gone back to Rwanda since 1994, and I was excited to see my family members who survived the genocide and learn about my biological parents and what happened to my country during the genocide. My uncle was nervous about me going back to Rwanda. He was concerned that I could be more traumatized, but after prayers and asking the Holy Spirit what to do, He asked me to go and promised to take care of me.

A few weeks later, I went to the Rwandan embassy in Pretoria to apply for my first Rwandan passport. I was warmly received by the staff, and they helped me fill out the documents. The lady who helped me assured that I would be contacted if they needed more information from me. I was told that it might take longer than expected because they needed to send my request to Rwanda. I was not worried because God told me that my passport would come sooner than I expected.

Two weeks after applying, I got a call from the embassy. They asked me to come back for an interview. I was very anxious and did not know what to tell them. The more I prayed, the more peace I felt about the interview. I felt peaceful and knew my South African family was supporting me and wanted to help me.

I went to Pretoria on the day of the interview with a family relative. When we arrived, I was asked to wait in a room for the person who would interview me. I prayed to God to favor me with the person who would oversee the interview. A man came into the room and introduced himself. He was genuine and made me feel comfortable as he started interviewing me. He asked how long I had been in South Africa and asked me to share my story. I told him how I had survived the genocide against the Tutsi in 1994 and how I ran away from the bondage of abuse and persecution. When I saw him entering the room, I knew that I could trust him and tell him the entire truth. I was not afraid of being misunderstood. I told him how I witnessed my father's death and how I had to forgive my relatives after finding out the truth about my father's death.

As I was sharing, I felt God's presence in the room. I knew God was with me and wanted me to tell him the entire truth to help me. When I finished sharing my story, the man excused himself for a moment and went outside. I rehearsed all the things I said and trusted that God was in control. The man came back with tears in his eyes and sat next to me. He said, "Aline, you have gone through many troubles, and I am so sorry for that. We are here for you and will protect you. You will get your passport and have a bright future ahead of you. I am so honored to have met you." I was surprised by the way God touched him and by his kind words. I left the embassy and felt grateful for God showing me that He would not allow me to go back to the land of oppression. Nothing was too big for Him.

While waiting for my passport, I started studying English and preparing for the IELTS (International English Language Testing System) examination. God provided the tuition fees for the English and the tools for my examination. He showed me that nothing could stop His promises by providing every step of the way.

A few months later, I was called by the embassy to collect my passport. The passport came earlier than expected as the Lord promised. It was the first Rwandan document I had ever had, and it felt good and peaceful to know that I would not have to go back to the country I had run from. I could turn the page completely. I started applying to universities, and my family told me not to apply to only one university as I had been told by the Holy Spirit. It was hard to argue with them because God had not yet healed my heart. I was pleasing people and wanted validation. I was willing to put aside whatever I had heard before getting my passport so I could be accepted.

One evening while praying, the Holy Spirit told me with a straight voice that I could not please men and Him at the same time. I had to choose who to obey. I decided to do as He said and only applied to the University of Pretoria. That was surprising to my family, especially my sisters. They thought I would study at the same university that they graduated from in Johannesburg.

I took a leap of faith and decided to apply to the university the Lord told me, where I would have to look for accommodations and be far from my family. I did not understand why God wanted me in Pretoria instead of Johannesburg with my sisters. I now understand why God took me to Pretoria instead of staying comfortable with my family in Johannesburg. While I was in Pretoria for my studies, my faith grew and was stretched to only look to God for every step I was taking. I grew spiritually, and I saw the hand and grace of God when making mistakes and receiving His help. I learned from my mistakes and pain and leaned on God for all my joy and peace. God used me to mentor other girls and grow out of my own desire and stretch toward serving God and not my own agenda. Pretoria was the place for training my soul. I was learning to trust God and stopped holding back from all the pain. In Pretoria, I learned to walk in freedom and experience the peace of God in all seasons.

When I got my admission letter to the University of Pretoria, I flew to Rwanda to apply for a student visa. I was not allowed to change my status from South Africa. I was excited to see my family who had survived the genocide, especially my uncle who attempted to rescue me. I was expectant about my trip because I knew that it would help me close the chapter of pain in my heart and forgive those who killed my father and other loved ones. I tried to forget about the man who killed my father and lived with me when I was with my grandmother, but could not do so on my own. I asked God to give me the strength to forgive him for killing my father. I came to understand that the only way I could forgive him would be to see the man who ordered him and his two brothers to kill my dad. The man was arrested after the genocide and was incarcerated in Butare (my hometown).

Many emotions were running through my mind as I prepared for my first trip to Rwanda. I realized that I needed to pause and rest in God's peace. I knew that God would go with me and every step I would take would be for my healing even when it ached at first.

On my way to the airport, I hugged my sisters and thanked them for their love and support. They had helped me with the application process and believed in me. I knew that going back to Rwanda would be different. I believed that God would heal the layers in my heart that were broken in the genocide. He would bring me back as a new person to pursue my studies in geology, as He promised, with a new heart and feelings healed from my past. I knew the trip was not just to get my visa. It was to close the door to my past by forgiving all the people who had hurt my family. I knew God was building my inner man to love and forgive what had happened in Rwanda.

I knew the only way to live a life of freedom was to let go of the hurt and forgive all the people I still held in my heart, especially the men behind my father's murder. After my grandmother told me the painful truth about the man who lived with us after we came from the refugee camp, I was deeply hurt. I did not forgive him or the other men involved. I knew God would help me release them because it was hard to do so. This trip would bring a deep healing and would connect me to the family member I did not know.

As mentioned in the second chapter, my biological parents were from two different tribes. I was raised with my mother's family who did not share much about the history of Rwanda because of their personal belief. I grew up not knowing my father's relatives who survived the genocide. I looked forward to meeting my surviving family members in Rwanda and hearing their stories.

CHAPTER 22
First Trip Back to Rwanda after the Genocide

I landed in Kigali (the capital of Rwanda) in the evening. Many family members came to the airport to welcome me. I had heard about most of them from speaking to my Uncle Jean who came to rescue me from the house of oppression. I was excited to meet them for the first time. When I saw my Uncle Jean, I ran to him and hugged him. I apologized for not saying goodbye to him when he came to rescue me. He was understanding and told me that he prayed for the day to come when I would be free. We left the airport and went to the house where I was going to stay.

Before my trip to Rwanda, the Holy Spirit asked me to get everyone a gift to thank them for having me and helping me take my life back. When we got to the house, I gave everyone their gifts and got to know them. Many family members came to welcome me and were happy to see me again. They had last seen me when I was four years old or younger. I did not remember any of the people except the uncle who came to rescue me.

After I gave everyone their gifts, some people asked me to share my experience of leaving the house of oppression. As I shared my story, they told me about how they had planned a rescue mission when my uncle and aunt came to see me. After hearing how they were all concerned about my situation, I knew that I was not alone. I was grateful that so many of my family members had survived the genocide and had many things to teach me. The atmosphere as we talked was heavy with emotion. It reminded them of memories that were still vivid in their minds, and my presence reminded them of my father since I looked like him.

After the talk, the visitors left. We went to bed because we were all tired. I was taken to my room, where I settled in and prepared for bed. I was relieved about how the first meeting went, and I could not wait to see how Rwanda looked the next day. My uncle could not show me the city because he was going back to his school that was a few hours away from the city. At that time, he was attending a seminary and was studying to become a Catholic priest.

Before I went to bed, my uncle gave me a gift that showed me how I was blessed to have him in my life. We spoke for a long time, and he told me that he prayed for this time to come to pass. I was touched by his kindness and knew I could trust him. Since I did not know how long I would be in Rwanda, I decided to make sure I saw all the family members who survived and reconnected myself with my history.

The following day, I was excited to start my discovery. My uncle offered to take me to see a few family members before he left. It was his last day before he went back to the seminary. After he left, I went out to visit the city.

I was excited to visit Kigali, and I met many people who knew my father. They had many stories to share with me, which made me feel close to my dad. After my grandmother passed away, I had no one else to tell me about my dad. By hearing their memories about my parents, I felt close to them and started to heal from their loss.

After a few days visiting family members, I went to visit the parents of the relatives I was staying with in Kigali. They lived in a small town outside the city. They were thrilled to see me and shared many stories about my father. I was happy to hear my father's deeds and was proud to be his daughter when I heard all the things he did in a short time and how he impacted many lives. I was very touched by their love and kindness. I had not seen such love and kindness after my grandmother passed away. I was happy to have grandparents again and family members I could look up to.

After the visit, I went to Kibungo (a town in the Eastern province of Rwanda), where I met my father's sister, Umulisa. She was very happy to meet me because she had last seen me when I was four years old. She was close to my father and met my mother before she passed away. When Umulisa saw me for the first time, she could not stop hugging me and crying. She felt like her brother was with her because I reminded her of him. I realized that she was still grieving my father's death. She had gone through traumatic events in the genocide. I spent the night with her, and she told me all the things she went through during the genocide. I started to build a close relationship with her and resolved to one day take her out of the environment she was living in so she could heal emotionally.

Unfortunately, I did not get to do much for her. She passed away while I was writing this book. I was devastated and remembered the promise I made to her that I would always try to make her proud. I realized that writing this book and finally finding healing would be the best things to do. In fact, when I heard that she had passed, I heard the Holy Spirit telling me to continue writing and not look back. That was hard because I did not get a chance to see her or go home for the funeral, but I knew God's will was for me to finish this book. The more I wrote, the more I could feel her looking down at me and cheering me on. The Bible states that we are surrounded by a great cloud of witnesses to cheer us on (Hebrews 12:1). Therefore I believed that she was cheering me on as I took the courage to write this book in spite of the grief of losing her.

After meeting my late aunt for the first time, I went to her father's house to see his grave. It was the only grave our family had of the people we lost in the genocide. Most of the family members who were killed in the genocide were not found. That grave represented all the loved ones who lost their lives, which was the reason for my visit.

As I stood in front of my grandfather's grave, two men came to greet us. When they left, I was told that they were responsible for my grandfather's death and were released after the Gacaca Court, the system that tried the people who were arrested after the genocide. I was filled with sadness and pain when I heard the news. I was angry and could not understand how they could kill my grandfather.

As I left my grandfather's house, I came to realize that I survived for a purpose. I decided to forgive the men who killed my grandfather because I knew they were driven by the enemy. I looked to God for the strength to do all I could do to make my parents proud and live a life of love and forgiveness. I was determined to do my best and work hard so I could help the people who survived, but did not have the same opportunities I had. Even though I went through my own pain and trials, I was fortunate to have gone to school and be given a chance to live in freedom. I realized that my success was not for me alone. It was for every survivor of any kind of pain and atrocity. I believe God delivered me so I could be a testimony of His grace and hope for my family. I went back to Kigali with a heavy heart and the determination to do all I could to be helpful and bring relief and hope to the people I met.

My uncle shared how my grandfather lost his life and how my grandmother was also killed at the Tanzanian border when she tried to cross the border. I also met some cousins from my father's side who survived the genocide. I was touched by their stories and was astonished by the heart of my uncle who took me in while he told me about all the atrocities he faced in the genocide. He had healed from the trauma and shared it as though it had happened to someone else. Many of my family relatives had learned to live with the pain and some found ways to heal.

As I listened to him, I prayed that one day I could share my story without feeling the pain. His faith and prayers helped him forgive the perpetrators for the pain felt. He told me that he chose to forgive the people who killed his father and learned to embrace them whenever he went to his father's house. I was starting to see the horror that my family faced in 1994 and how unthinkable it was not to be traumatized and not to be broken. It was hard for me to forgive at that moment because I was exposed to the truth and could see how much pain they went through during their walk to survival.

My uncle encouraged me to forgive the people who killed our family members. He stated that hatred would not be beneficial to me and would hurt me even more. I did not know how I could forgive after hearing the truth about my grandparents' deaths and my father's death, but I trusted that God would heal my brokenness.

My heart was broken for the third time, and I did not know how I would find the strength to move on and completely let go of the pain I felt when I met the men who killed my grandfather as my uncle did. I was shocked and touched by his heart's posture, and I asked God to help me forgive and forget all the pain that hurt my loved ones.

On our way back, the Holy Spirit whispered to me that this trip was the beginning of my healing. I needed to know the truth before He could heal me completely. I did not understand what he meant at that time because I was very emotional and could not think wisely. As I look back on my trip to my grandfather's house, I realize how God took me to the darkest part of my past to heal me and take the root of sorrow from my life. That way, I could share this with you without being traumatized again.

God has the perfect time to heal us. For me, it took eighteen years before He allowed me to go back to my country and hear the atrocities my family endured. He knew that my heart was ready to go through the healing process. I was filled with many questions as I heard how some of my relatives were killed. I did not know why I survived and why God protected me and let others be killed.

Before I went to Rwanda, part of me always wondered why my family in Rwanda did not look for me before I was abused. However, after my trip to my grandfather's house, I realized they had gone through much worse and needed time to heal before they could look for me.

A few days after coming back from my grandfather's house, I went to meet another uncle who was also my father's brother and lived in the Northern Province of Rwanda. I was excited to meet him because I had heard many wonderful things about him. I realized that few of my father's siblings had survived and were all grateful to see me after many years. I was happy to meet him for the first time and felt at home as I met his family.

After I visited every family member who was alive, I was left with going back to the town where I was born and where my father was killed. I was very stressed because I wondered what I would find out by going back to the place where my father lost his life. I knew the first thing I needed to do was meet the man who ordered his brother to kill my father because he was incarcerated in one of the prisons in town.

When I told my family about my intention to meet the man who ordered my dad's death, they were against it. They tried to protect me because they thought I would be more traumatized if I met him. Only my Uncle Jean agreed with me. He explained to them how it would be a healing process for me when I meet him. They finally agreed because I asked for it as a birthday gift because I needed it to heal and believed the only way to heal would be to forgive him when I saw him. One of my uncles requested a visit to the prison for October 19, 2012, the day before my birthday.

On that day, we drove to my hometown with two of my father's siblings and a cousin. That was a historic moment because no one in my family had done it. They were all worried that I would come back even more traumatized. We drove for three hours, and I prayed in my heart for God's will to be done when we got there. We had to stop at the house where I lived with my father. It was the last place I saw my father alive and hid under the bed. I also wanted to meet the man who helped arrest the man in prison. He was his brother and also a friend of my father. The Holy Spirit had asked me to give him a gift to thank him for sending the man to prison.

When we arrived in Butare (my hometown), we went to the house where my parents lived. I wanted to first heal from the last memories I had from the house before I could meet the man who ordered my father's death. I found out that other people were living inside. Therefore, we could not get in, but we took pictures of the outside and the entrance of the house. I did not have any vivid memory of the house, but I felt a river of emotions as I stood outside the house. I remembered the last time I was inside the house and the last memories I had of my father. I could not remember anything prior to the day of his death. It was very touching, and I tried to stop my tears so my uncles wouldn't stop me from going to the prison.

After seeing my parents' house, we spent time with family friends who hadn't seen me since a few days before my dad was killed. They were all in tears because I reminded them of my father in so many ways. Some shared how they had been impacted by my father. I was grateful that my father lived an impactful life, and I promised myself to do my best to follow in his footsteps and impact people around me. I was proud of being his daughter. That was another confirmation that God allowed me to survive because He had a greater plan for me. I just needed to let it unfold.

After sharing the stories and greeting the neighbors and friends of my dad, I went to meet the man who sent his brother to prison. As I walked toward him, I could feel the tension around me. My uncles did not want me to meet him. I gave him his gift and thanked him for giving justice to my father's death and the deaths of many people who his brother ordered him to kill. He hugged me and told me that sorry he was when he heard that my father had been killed. They had been friends and traveled together before the genocide started. Before meeting him, I was asked not to tell him that I was on my way to meet his brother in jail for safety reasons. After greeting him and thanking him, we drove to the prison. The director of the prison was waiting to speak to us before we met the man.

On the way, I started wondering what I would tell him and how I would ask him where they put my father's body. No one knew where they left him after they killed him, and his body was never found. I wanted to ask him where he left my dad's body so I could go and close that chapter of my grieving. I also wanted to put a face on the man who took my father away from me. After meeting all those people, I did not know how I would phrase my questions without crying. I also wondered what his reaction would be when he saw that the little girl, he had ordered the three men to kill, was still alive.

We were escorted to the prison by a good friend of my father, who was well-known throughout Rwanda because of his work. I was happy to meet with him because he told me many good things about my dad. He also asked why I wanted to see the man who killed my dad, and I told him what I had in my heart. He was a very genuine man and listened to me. He told me that the director of the prison wanted to meet us. My request was not common, and they needed to make sure I would not be more traumatized after I met him. After the conversation, he drove me to the prison.

As we parked in front of the prison, my father's friend asked me to let him explain my intentions to the director. We were gladly welcomed by the director. He knew my father's friend and was happy to meet me. The director asked me how I came about deciding to meet a man who did the worst thing a child can face. I told him how I lived with one of the men who killed my father and could not stop thinking about the pain my father faced. I wanted to know where they put my father's body after they took his life. After I heard that the man who ordered the murder was arrested, I decided to meet him so I could forgive him and the other three men involved. I decided to step in faith and meet the man so I could let go of all the questions I had. I had carried the anger and frustration for many years, and I was ready to forgive and step into my destiny. As I answered the director, I could feel the presence of God and His peace within me. I knew that I would not come out more traumatized from the meeting. I would be healed and ready to embrace my future.

The director looked at me and said, "Your reasons are far beyond what I expected. However, I cannot let you see him alone and introduce yourself to him because he has people outside the prison that can harm you. I will call him to my office and have a chat with him while you are here, and you will be able to see him as you wish without saying a word. Is that fine?" I agreed, and he sent an officer to get the man.

My heart was in turmoil, and I could not feel my body. I started wondering if he would remember me and know who I was, but as I started to worry, I heard the soft voice of the Holy Spirit telling me that I was covered and hidden in Him. Nothing would harm me. I was relieved and waited for him in peace. I knew that God would strengthen me.

A few minutes later, an old man came in wearing a pink jail uniform. He looked very angry and tired. He seemed to be in his late fifties and had a dark face that remains in my head to this day. He sat down and greeted us with a nod. The director introduced us as people doing research in agriculture who wanted to hear about his rice harvest. The prisoners had many projects, and one of them was agriculture. When he heard this, he talked about his harvest, how that year was great. He told us what his plans were for the next season, and he was confident that the results would be better if they continued at the same pace. He also mentioned how hard it was to work since he had a heart disease, which he was taking treatments for.

As the man shared his project, my mind wrestled and many memories resurfaced. I was thinking of all the pain he caused to families who lost loved ones because of his orders. When the man mentioned about his health issues, I stopped thinking in the trend I was and listened more carefully. I realized it was worthless not to forgive him because he was facing the consequences of his actions. My heart was no longer cold towards him, but filled with compassion and hope that he would encounter God. It was not my battle to fight anymore. I knew God would fight for all the families who lost loved ones because of his orders. I prayed in my heart and asked God to give me the strength to forgive him and let go of my pain toward him and his brothers. As I prayed, I felt a deep pain in my heart. It felt like surgery was being done in my heart, and I started to see him differently.

Before the prisoner finished sharing about his rice harvest to the director, he proudly acknowledged his father's name. His father was one of the orchestrators and the brains of the genocide's ideology. When I heard his father's name, I felt nauseous. I wanted to scream at the top of my lungs, but I held my tongue because I did not want him to recognize me.

The director concluded the chat and asked the officer to take him back to his cell. When he left, the office was silent. Everyone was processing what they had heard. We all wondered what this man would do if he was released because he did not look ashamed of his past decisions. He seemed proud to associate himself with the man behind the genocide's ideology.

The director broke the silence and asked how I felt when I saw him. I told him how my mind was replaying all the things I was told about him. I chose to let go of my anger and hatred against him because I realized God was fighting for me though I could not see it then. They did not understand my decision, and my uncles were angrier than before. After the meeting, I felt lighter and more peaceful, but my cousin and uncles were taken back to the past. They remembered many things that man did with his power and all the people he ordered killed in Butare. The director told me that he had not been given a life sentence and would be out in twelve years. It was frightening to me that he was not remorseful for his actions. However, after praying, I realized that God was in control. I had to give it to God and trust that he would have his way with the future of the man. I apologized to my uncles and cousin for reminding them about how their brother and uncle had been killed.

For me, the prison was a place of deliverance. I went home freer than ever. I was a different person after I met the man who took my father's life. Although my questions were not answered, I felt peace because I could now grieve my father and heal. I was not done grieving my father, but I was done hating the people who hurt him. My family members were not ready to forgive him yet. I prayed for them and gave them to God because I knew their time of healing would come too.

As we left the prison, my smile came back. It felt like the sun was rising in my life. I was no longer in the darkness. I was walking in the light of my Savior. My heart was thankful for allowing me to move on, and I looked forward to a brighter future in God.

We were invited by more friends of my father to celebrate my birthday before driving back to Kigali. The director had asked us not to sleep over in town for my safety. I met the brother of my father's fiancée who was killed a few days before my father. Her brother told me great things about his sister and my father; she loved me and had the same name as my mother, which was very surprising to me. They told me about how much I loved spending time with her and that my dad was very happy I would have a mother who would love me. My father was always looking after me, and this brought a lot of tears to my eyes.

My twenty-fourth birthday marked the beginning of my walk to healing and discovery of who I truly was in Christ. I started to rise above my failures and the insecurities of my past. I decided to move forward with no hindrances from my past. I prayed that God would use my past to bring glory to His name.

On our way back to Kigali, I thanked God for allowing us to meet the man in prison and for leaving my burdens and anger there. I was grateful to have met people who knew my father. It made me see how my father had left a great legacy behind him by impacting all who knew him.

As I was praying, the Holy Spirit told me that I would write a book to share all the experiences I had gone through. Many people would find hope in the trials and pain they have faced. When I heard Him say that I would write a book, I did not believe it at first. I did not share it with anybody because I did not feel like my story would ever bring hope to someone. However, I realized it was not my work to understand how sharing my story would bring hope. I was called to obey and write truthfully about all the events. God would give me the strength I needed to write and touch the hearts of readers. I did not believe that I would sit down five years later and write it on my own with God by my side.

The five years were not wasted. They were unfolding the layers of healing that needed to be done so I could see myself the way God sees me and be confident in Him so I could achieve what he told me in the car on our way back from meeting the man behind my father's death. In those five years, I achieved my academic dreams of being a geologist. I also discovered my purpose of being an advocate for Christ by sharing the goodness of His healing power over my life, which led to writing this book. Even though God started to heal parts of my past in 2012, I was still ashamed about what I had gone through. I needed to break away from the shame and embrace who I had become because of the pain so I could share it. I had to rise above my brokenness and discover my worth and the purpose of the pain. The process did not take a day or weeks; it took years.

Today, I am thankful for those years. They were not wasted, and they gave me new perspectives on my pain and trials. I can fully testify that Romans 8:28 is truly working in my life because all my pain, rejection, survival, and abuse worked together to make me the woman I am today. I am so grateful for who I have become, and I do not have any regrets about my past. God turned my ashes into beauty, and I wouldn't want it any other way.

CHAPTER 23
Back to School

After visiting my family members and traveling around Rwanda, I proceeded to apply for the South African student visa to go back and study geology. I was excited to finally pursue the career I had always wanted, surrounded by people who loved me and wanted the best for me. I wanted to pursue my dreams so I could be helpful with my expertise and supply water to remote areas of Africa. I believed God had called me to minister to the people through my work and was ready to study hard to bring a change in the world.

I got my student visa, went back to South Africa, and moved to Pretoria. God provided for my tuition fees and accommodation, which was a miracle on its own. I knew God wanted me in Pretoria for a purpose. I was ready to trust Him in the process because I knew He had my best interests in mind.

As I was looking for an apartment, God gave me the best choice and kept me there until I finished school and graduated. I could see His hands in everything I did. Before we started the semester, I was reminded of how four years back I dreamed of studying geology and was not given the opportunity. I studied organic chemistry, which was not my first choice, but it was the only way I could study at the university where I was enrolled. I was about to study geology, and my heart was filled with great joy because my time had finally come to step into my dream.

I looked for a roommate for my first year in Pretoria and met a beautiful girl who was South African. I loved living with her. We had different majors, but we got along very well. We enjoyed living together and grew spiritually since she too was a Christian. I realized that God had not only brought me in Pretoria for my studies; it was to make disciples in His name. With my background in organic chemistry, I was asked to tutor freshmen students. I took the opportunity to talk about Jesus. I came to be known as the Christian tutor, and my friends would ask for prayers and help with their academics.

Since I was fortunate to have my fees paid off, I was determined to finish my degree in time and start working to help my family back in Rwanda. I knew it was not my burden to carry, but I was always reminded of how privileged I was to study and be a college student when my peers did not finish high school. This gave me more determination to be the light to my family members who were not all saved.

My college years were summarized in two words: work and prayer. I was very involved in church and had no time to socialize. My studies were my priorities. It opened doors to tutoring math, chemistry, and structural geology. I helped many classmates with love and shared the Word of God when I could.

Even though I was sharing God's Word and promises, I had never shared my full story because I was still filled with shame. I was not fully healed because many parts were still unfolding and God was healing me little by little. The devil made me believe that nothing good could come from sharing my story. No one knew I was a survivor of abuse and genocide. I did not even share it with my close college friends because I was ashamed of my story. I wanted to be validated and loved by many, and I was always trying to compare myself to my surroundings. I tried to be what they wanted me to be, but I lost myself in the process. My story was too sad to share. I could not show the goodness of God because I had not fully owned my past or healed from it.

I rejected myself inwardly, and I felt rejected in some of my relationships because I could not be open with people because I feared their judgment. I did not let myself become vulnerable around the people I loved because I was scared of losing them. Although I was loved and surrounded by many people, I was not able to tell them what happened to me as a child and a teenager. Part of me did not want to be portrayed as a victim if they found out I was an orphan who had been abused by a relative.

I chose to work hard and build a new Aline that people could relate to. I tried to bury the old me by hiding. I was not ready to face my fears and step out of my pain. I decided to keep my story to myself and my family. I was striving for success and the validation of others, believing that it would fill the void in my heart and give me a sense of peace and joy.

After two years of serving faithfully in the church where I was plugged in, God took me out after a season of persecution. I knew persecution was normal for a child of God, but I could not find the peace to be still and not feel wounded when I was taken out of the church. I realized God was showing me a trend that He wanted to break in me.

I thought the persecution was only due to my devotion for God and an attack from the enemy. However, as I was digging deeper and praying for God to give me more revelation, I came to see that my desire to be validated and loved was reflecting in the church community. God took me out because He wanted me to seek Him alone and not do things to be validated and accepted in the church. I realized I needed to look up to Him and not look around me to seek what people wanted me to do. The more I would pray and seek God, the more I would see that I needed to let go of my fear and embrace my story and my testimony.

I went back to the source of all my joy, my heavenly Father, and poured out my heart to Him. I was tired of running away from myself and building a wall that was not protecting me from pain. It was giving me more pain. As I prayed for help, I understood there was a purpose for my story. God gave me the courage to share it with a close friend from school, and she told me that God would use my story to minister to other women as He did to her. As I shared my story with my friend, I realized how God was using her to remind me of the power of my story. It was no longer mine to hide. She stated that God would use it to heal other women, and He would heal me first. I was very humbled when she said those words. I knew that I had to let God heal me first.

I had to stop running from the healing, and I had to running toward my fears so God could heal me.

I pursued my studies while seeking God. I graduated as a geologist and was on my way to becoming the person I always dreamed of being. I was excited to provide an answer for the African countries that struggle to supply pure water to their population. I allowed God to heal every layer of my life, which required vulnerability.

The first step in healing was taking me back to the time of abuse and healing the hidden parts that I kept to myself. I realized that I was not responsible for what happened to me. I had believed for a time that I was responsible for what my relative did to me, and I could not forgive myself for allowing it to happen. I always kept it in my heart and never shared it to anybody. Since God knew my heart, He started by healing the guilt that was in my heart. This process took weeks of praying and spending time in His presence.

The second step was realizing that my achievement was driven by many factors from my past. I wanted to erase the pain from my mind by showing myself that I could be successful and forget all I had gone through by focusing on material things, which impacted my desire to be loved, be validated by society, and no longer feel like an outcast. As the Holy Spirit revealed this to me, I was undone. I cried out to God to heal me and help me see myself the way He sees me and loves me. I asked Him to show me my identity in Him because I no longer knew who I truly was. I was consumed by the opinions of others.

God showed me the parts of my heart that needed healing, and He started to heal them in layers. He asked me to forgive all the people who had hurt me and give them to Him. I believed I had forgiven many of them, but in the presence of God, I realized I had many wounds that were still bleeding because I had not completely forgiven them. I asked God to change my heart and give me a heart that would love again.

> *"I will give you a new heart and put a new spirit in you;*
> *I will remove from you your heart of stone and give you a*
> *heart of flesh." (Ezekiel 36:26)*

As I was letting go of the offenses and the hurtful words people had said over me, I felt lighter. I realized it was not my place to hate them. I was to pray and intercede for them, and God would fight for me.

I realized that God had started to fight for me when I stepped out of myself and gave it to Him. The people who said I was a false prophet had started to face difficult consequences. When I heard this, my heart was saddened. God had started to fight for me. I tried to intercede for some Christians who offended me, and the Holy Spirit gave me 1 Chronicles 16:22 (NKJV): "Do not touch my anointed ones, and do my prophets no harm."

Some people came to apologize for their actions before I left Pretoria, which made me realize that God was my defender and advocate. I forgave them and let Him fight my battles.

After forgiving others and letting go of the offensive words in my heart, it was time to forgive myself for the things I believed when I was going through rejection and the choices I made when I was looking to fill the void in my heart. I had found myself doing things that I never thought I would do because of the fear of being alone. I was in relationships that were not growing my spirituality, and I was afraid to let go because I was comfortable. That step was the hardest to take.

In some of my decisions, I was the only one who was aware of the pain. I knew God was not pleased with those decisions, but I chose them anyway. I had to confess those decisions to God and ask for forgiveness. I forgave myself for all the wrong decisions I made, which shut down the enemy's lies that I had allowed to speak over my life. It was hurtful and shameful to realize I did not know my worth as a woman.

I needed to let go of my insecurities and be redefined by God's love and mercy. I thought I had so much sin that it was hard for me to be whole again, but God reminded me that His grace was enough for me.

One night, I woke up because I felt a hand touching my back. I switched on the light and was surprised to see there was nothing behind me. I prayed and heard a soft voice saying, "Lamentations 3:22-23."

I stood up, took my Bible, and read: "Because of the Lord's great love we are not consumed, for his compassions never fail."

I felt the Holy Spirit touching my heart and pouring God's love into my heart. I could not stop rejoicing about His mercy and grace over me. I read that His mercies are renewed every morning, and I realized there was nothing too big or too bad for the blood of Jesus and His mercy to wash away. From that revelation, I knew that I did not have to worry. Every day brought new mercy for every step of my life. As I was reading the scripture, I realized my search for love and validation was useless because I was loved by the Father. His love would never fail me and would make me whole as I embraced Him with all my heart.

We all face times when we feel lost and unworthy of going back to the arms of God. You may be in this situation and feel like you can relate to me. I would like to remind you that there is no sin that is too bad for God to forgive. He will welcome you into His arms. He is your Father, and He will never leave you or forsake you even when you fall and stray from Him.

Sometimes the enemy reminds us about what we did in the past to stop us from going toward God and embracing His love. The devil's scheme is to bring a seed of shame to your life and maximize your sins, but God already forgave you as you confess your sins to Him. He wants you to draw near to Him so you can experience His freedom. Everything the enemy uses against us is to make us feel unworthy of God's love and forgiveness, but His love and forgiveness are always available to us. We should always remember that Jesus died for us while we were still sinners, and He would never reject us. As we go to the throne of grace and receive the mercies that are renewed for us every morning, we have to fight the condemnation of the devil and walk a life of freedom. Whoever the Son sets free is free indeed.

As you read these lines, the devil wants you to feel condemned and regret what you did in the past. He wants you to feel sorry for yourself and live your life as a victim when you can live a victorious life in Christ Jesus. When Jesus comes into your life, He takes away all your shame and guilt, and He gives you joy for your troubles.

I had to face my shame and guilt to realize that God only wanted me to live a life free of shame and guilt. I can love my neighbor as I love myself. I realized I could not love others if I did not love myself and embrace my identity in Jesus Christ. There is no condemnation for those who are in Jesus Christ (Romans 8:1). I finally understood that God could not heal me when I was in a state of denial. I needed Jesus to take away my sins and give me a new garment because I was wearing garments of shame, guilt, and low self-esteem. I gave Him my heart and repented for all the sins, known and unknown, that were blocking me from receiving complete healing. I welcomed His mercy and grace into my life and realized that life without Him was impossible and worthless.

The process of deep healing took time because God wanted to heal every part of my soul that needed healing. In October 2017, I had a heavenly encounter and realized that God was setting me free from all generational curses and the bondage that had followed me since birth. On October 13, 2017, I finally was delivered and could share my testimony without guilt or shame. After the deliverance and healing, God put in my heart that the next step was to write this book. It was no longer frightening to me because He had delivered me from shame and rejection. I was ready to share everything without fearing the outcome. After my deliverance, I was asked to speak at a women's conference and share my story, which I did for the first time in front of women I did not know. That was stressful at first, but I realized God was giving me the words to say, and that built my confidence. After the first few words, I realized God was giving me the boldness to share my story. I saw the impact it had on the women at the conference, which gave me the peace to write this book.

I knew God wanted me to write it on my own, but I did not know how long this would take because I had no background in writing. I stood up in faith and believed that God would give me the skills required to write it. Even though I did not know how to start, I chose to obey His Word because I knew He would see me through it.

CHAPTER 24
Difficulties

After stepping in faith to write the book, I went through many difficulties. One of the most painful was the loss of my Aunt Umulisa. She was very dear to my heart. I had grown close to her in 2012 when we were united again in Rwanda. Her passing brought a lot of pain because I could not attend her funeral. That was a hard time because I was far from my family and was grieving her death alone, but the grieving season was quickly stopped by God when the Holy Spirit reminded me of my assignment because He wanted me to focus on writing the book.

In fact, when I heard that Umulisa had passed away, I was in complete shock. The Holy Spirit told me to write and not take a break. I did not understand why I could not take the time to grieve like everyone else in a similar situation, but I realized that the more I grieved, the lonelier I would feel. The feelings that God healed me from would want to resurface. I realized that God was not against me grieving my aunt. He was protecting me from the spirit of grief coming into my life and stopping my assignment. I obeyed and woke up every morning to write until I could not feel my hands. I wrote this book by hand because my computer crashed when I decided to start writing the book. The more I wrote, the more I would find peace about her passing. I received the comfort of the Holy Spirit. He is our present help in times of pain.

The pain became a pushing tool to finish the book because God had given me the vision behind this book. He told me that it would help many people find healing in Him. I knew my aunt had gone home to be with her heavenly Father and would not want to come back if given the chance because she was finally healed from all the pain. I knew she was with Jesus because she called His name as she passed away, which confirmed Romans 10:13 (NKJV): "For whoever calls on the name of the Lord shall be saved." That gave me the confirmation that even though I did not get a chance to say goodbye, I would see her again and would rejoice with her in the presence of Jesus.

A part of me was broken because I wanted to do many things with her before she went to heaven, but I was assured that she was resting in the presence of the Lord. I gave my pain to God and trusted He would heal me and give me the strength to write this chapter as He asked me to do.

A few months before my aunt passed away, I had an open vision while I was praying. I saw myself walking on road, and Jesus was holding my right hand. The road was filled with thorns and I was walking on them. I could see the blood on my feet, but I could not feel the pain. My eyes were on Jesus as I walked with Him holding my right hand. I knew it was Jesus because I had had previous visions of Him. His eyes were full of fire and everlasting love for me. He was dressed in a white robe and a golden belt. He looked just like the first vision I had of Him in my bedroom before I was freed from the abuse. I could see the holes in His hand as He held my hand and walked with me.

As I walked with Jesus, the road was lonely and filled with big thorns that wounded my feet, but the thorns only hurt when I looked down at them and lost focus on Jesus' eyes. I could walk with Jesus through the thorns without feeling any pain when I looked at Jesus, but as soon as I looked down, the pain made it hard to walk.

After I passed the road of thorns, I looked back. The thorns had disappeared and turned into green grass. In front of me, women were waiting for me. They were hurt and broken and had lost their identity just as I had. When they saw me and Jesus walking toward them, they took off their filthy garments and started walking with Jesus on their side. They were dressed with new robes as they walked. I did not stop walking with Jesus when I saw them. The women walked behind us with shouts of joy and helped other women take off their dirty garments and follow us.

I walked hand in hand with Jesus and climbed a mountain. When I turned back for the second time, the grass was greener. As I walked forward with Jesus, the number of women increased. When we arrived at the top of the mountain, Jesus asked me to look behind me, and He said, "This will be your legacy, Aline." With that, the vision was over.

As I prayed and asked God for the interpretation of the vision, I came to understand that my walk with Jesus will have many difficulties. It may feel lonely at times. However, I should remember that Jesus is holding my hand and walking alongside me. This vision also showed that the walk will bring many wounds, but if I fix my eyes on Jesus, the pain will not stop me from fulfilling the calling on my life. I remembered that in the vision I did not feel the pain as I looked to Jesus, but only felt it when I looked down.

The wounds will be a testimony to many and encourage many to walk with Christ and find their identity in Christ. In the interpretation, the Holy Spirit said that the road of thorns was the pain, trials, and persecutions that were to come. Despite the pain, I will be growing spiritually as I walk with Him. He assured me that He will not leave me, nor will He forsake me. Even though the road may feel lonely, I will not be alone. Jesus will be walking with me. The blood on my feet as I walked was the blood of Jesus. It covered my feet through the pain. Even though I may be wounded on the way, I will be able to bear the pain. Jesus will take all my pain, and nothing will harm me (Psalm 91). As the Holy Spirit gave me the interpretation of the vision, I was comforted to know that Jesus was holding my hand during my walk. I knew that as I seek God, trials and difficulties may arise.

I wrote down the interpretation of the vision five months before I lost my aunt, but I did not realize the season had already started. I needed to keep walking even when it hurt. I was reminded of the vision when the Holy Spirit told me not to stop writing and to focus on Him and not on the loss. My purpose was greater than what I could see. I believe God gave me the vision to remind me that my walk is not for myself. It is to help other women find the Creator and live lives of purpose. Every night, I was reminded of the women who were waiting for me to go through the road of thorns and get to them so they could take off their dirty garments and walk in freedom. I realized it was not about me. I needed to rise above my pain and grief and write even when I felt no desire to do so.

God wanted me after receiving the vision, to surrender my life and hold His hand as He guides me to the women who need His healing and restoration. From that day, I knew my purpose would be fulfilled as I let Him direct my path and fix my eyes on Him. I decided to walk hand in hand with Jesus no matter the outcome. In fact, He already prepared us for the trouble in John 16:33:

> *"I have told you these things, so that in me you may have peace. In this world you will have trouble, but take heart! I have overcome the world."*

As I meditated on this scripture, I realized that all godly assignments would bring great trials and persecution. Jesus told His disciples that they would face trials and tribulations as they do the works they were called to do and this applies to all Christians. I knew that releasing this book was not only to share the goodness of God to readers, but to also allow them to arise and walk with Jesus no matter the cost and pain.

I also came to understand that walking hand in hand with Christ sometimes requires isolation. Jesus went at times to lonely places to seek His Father. I realized seasons of isolation are not punishments. In contrary, they draw us to God, and we become dependent on His presence.

I had to find joy in God and not expect to be always surrounded by people in my walk with Him. In the Bible, God always met His people in lonely places. Moses was in exile for forty years and was tending his father-in-law's flock when he was led into the wilderness to encounter God (Exodus 3:1). On Mount Horeb, Moses was alone with the flock when the angel of God gave him his assignment to rescue the children of Israel from bondage. He discovered his purpose when he was alone in the wilderness. God isolated Moses so he could focus and hear Him.

We all need to hear God for ourselves, and for that to occur, we need to find a personal time and place where we are all alone with God and wait to hear from Him. God is always speaking; to hear Him, we need to be in tune with the Holy Spirit.

As I saw the vision and heard its interpretation, I was filled with great expectations about what God would do through my vulnerability. Although I knew pain would come along the way, I was filled with peace because I was assured that Jesus would take me through it. God was building my character and stretching me so that in due time I could help others. I knew that I would not be shaken as I look up to Him, and I will keep walking in spite of the trouble and pain.

When I faced pain while writing this book, 2 Corinthians 4:8-9 kept me going:

> *We are hard pressed on every side but not crushed; perplexed,*
> *but not in despair; persecuted, but not abandoned; struck*
> *down, but not destroyed.*

In these verses, Paul came to understand there was a cost to pay when we walk with Christ, but we should not lose hope because we cannot be destroyed. When I heard the Holy Spirit telling me to write when I was in pain, I realized it was not new because Paul wrote in spite of the circumstances he faced. In prison, he wrote many letters to the churches he founded (Ephesians, Philippians, Colossians, and Philemon). Paul did not stop ministering to the church when he was in chains. In fact, he wrote more letters to the church in prison than when he was free. Paul was not looking out for his own needs. He decided to edify others when he was in chains and isolated instead of feeling sorry for himself and fall in despair. Therefore, we must set our eyes on God and on what is unseen. Our circumstance sometimes wants to bring us down when we are called to move forward with God. We cannot stop walking when we face trouble and pain. In fact, pain can bring out the best in us, and it has power to grow us and stretch us to the capacity God intended us to grow into.

In my time of grief, I wrote more chapters than I wrote while I was happy and surrounded by people. For this book to be written, God had to take me deeper to squeeze out all that was inside me. God reminded me that I was no longer living for myself but was living for Jesus who lives within me. He also told me that this book was not mine, but His.

After realizing this was not my book, that God was using my story to heal others, every page brought light to my heart as I wrote. I looked past my own needs and reminded myself of the women in my vision and how my walk with Jesus mattered for their healing. I was ready to come out of my comfort zone and come out of the wilderness. I believe God can use my story to bring healing to every person who reads this book. I grew through every painful experience, so that God could use it and I could write this book for His glory.

The pain faced while writing this book did not destroy me. I did not only lose my aunt, but also faced betrayal and rejection in relationships. This did not overtake me, but made me better. I could rely on God alone to take me through it so I could be a living testimony for everyone reading this book. I realized pain was not a punishment from God. It was a tool God used to bring out the best in us and grow our inner selves. Jesus faced the greatest pain by bringing salvation and redemption for all. We can walk in assurance that we will never face the pain alone because we have a Savior who will strengthen us in times of pain.

I am so grateful for the great moments I spent with my Aunt Umulisa, who was always supportive and gave me all the love she could give whenever I was with her. She always told me about how much my parents loved each other and how much they loved me. She also had a traumatic story about the genocide that shaped her for the rest of her life. I was grateful to share my story with her before she passed away. I miss her so much, but I know she is at peace and enjoying her time with the Lord.

CHAPTER 25
Main Goal

Before the Holy Spirit asked me to write this book in 2017, He showed me the vision of the women who were waiting for me at the end of the thorny road. He went on and told me that this book will bring restoration, freedom, and peace of mind to every person who reads it. I realized this book was bigger than everything I ever dreamed or thought.

God started to remind me of how Moses was sent to Egypt to rescue the Israelites from bondage. Moses was not a well-spoken person and had low self-confidence. God chose him to deliver His people so all the glory would be His, and He used what Moses had in his hand: his staff (Exodus 4:1-2). As I studied the story of Moses, I realized that we live in a world where many people are living in the bondage of pain and hurt. God asked me to write this book so He can free His people who read it with expectation and who rely on Him.

Our world is filled with wounded people who need healing and restoration. This is sometimes unknown to many of us who encountered Christ, found hope and joy in our suffering, and understood that pain is necessary and inevitable. As I wrote this book, I was reminded of all the men and women who fall into depression and hopelessness. They do not know how to process the pain they are facing, and they believe the lies, that the enemy whispers to them.

I came to understand that God wanted to complete His healing in me as I wrote each chapter. I went back into my memories and remembered all the things I had overcome with Him so that He could bring healing for people who had similar paths or wounds. They need to be reminded that they are not forgotten and can heal and live peaceful lives. You don't need to have a story similar to mine for God to heal you and free you. Any pain you face or have gone through can be healed and used to help others.

Some people told me that my story was very sad. They felt like their pain was smaller than mine. I completely disagree. Pain is relative, and all pain matters to God if it matters to you. We all have different paths of life, and the world today pushes us to compare our walks and paths with others. We are unique, and our pain is unique to us. I encourage you not to undermine your story and allow God to heal you where you need healing.

By sharing my story and all the fears and pain I overcame, I want to show readers that they can face any pain life brings and come out stronger than ever. Knowing someone who went through an analogous situation and came out on the other side gives us hope that we can do the same thing. This happened to me when I listened to the testimonies of other women who had painful pasts. Many went through similar pain and rejection, but they were healed and were used by God to empower women and help them overcome their pain. Listening to other testimonies helped me understand how my pain had a purpose. I began to believe that I could come out of bondage, live a free life, and come out stronger and more hopeful for a better future. It gave me hope to believe that I could come out of the house of oppression and it happened as I believed.

Before I could share my story, I had to go through personal healing. God healed every layer of my heart little by little. I encourage you to let God heal every layer of your heart as He reminds you of events, which you may have forgotten, so you may be free. We all need healing in our lives in one way or another. The first step is acknowledging that we are broken and looking inside our lives with truthfulness. Sometimes we do not heal because we are still in denial about the pain.

If you are reading this, I believe there is a part of your life that needs healing. This may be lost confidence, pain you faced in the past, rejection, or abuse etc. God can bring healing to every area of your life just as He did for me. He will give you a new identity in Him, and He will restore all the things the enemy stole from you. Before God can heal you, you need to surrender your life to Him, as I did, and stop running to temporary solutions. You need to trust that He can heal you.

Open your heart to experience freedom in all areas of your life. Some may not relate to my testimony as you read it, but you may have pains or trials in your life that made you feel distressed or anxious. God wants to heal all the pain that is coming to your mind as you read this. You can live a life of freedom. It may be bondage over sin, addiction, or other things that take up your mind and keep you awake at night.

Sometimes the bondage one faces is seeking validation from others. I tried to please people so I could be loved, but I came to understand that the only thing that matters is to know that God loves me. That was more than enough for me and it can be the same for you. You may have tried all you know to do to find love and peace, but the void in your heart can only be filled by God's love and presence. He created you, and only He can fill it.

Being in bondage is having limited rights and the power to change oneself. In fact, you may live in bondage without being aware of it if sin is a normal habit and you do not have any remorse when you sin. The word *sin* means missing the mark. When you live life below what God has planned for you and are comfortable in it, you may be living in bondage. If you always live as a victim, live in self-pity, or always find excuses not to do the things of God, it may be the bondage God wants to free you from.

The term *bondage* is used for *slaves*, but when I was writing this book, God told me that many who would read it cannot move forward because they are slaves to sin and trapped in the pain of their past, just as I was. God does not want us to live in our failures and pain; He wants to heal us and give us the freedom that only He can give. Jesus came down from heaven to earth to set us free and break every chain in our lives (such as sexual immorality, alcohol or drug addictions, unforgiveness, unworthiness, past hurts, generational curses, etc.).

The process of healing may take time, but the first step is recognizing that you need healing. You need to welcome God into your heart to reveal what needs healing. Some parts may be unknown to us, but God can reveal them if we draw near to Him.

The second step is repentance:

If we confess our sins, he is faithful and just and will forgive our sins and purify us from all unrighteousness. (1 John 1:9)

God is waiting for us to confess all the sins that He will reveal to us and pour out our pain to Him. All the sins that hold you down and make you ashamed need to be confessed because God is faithful and will forgive you and renew you. Repentance was the very first message that Jesus shared in the beginning of His ministry. In fact, after being in the wilderness for forty days and being tempted by the devil, Jesus started preaching about repentance (Matthew 4:17). We live in a world where repentance is no longer common. The word *repentance* means a turn of heart and mindset. This means that as we repent to God, we turn our hearts away from the sin we repented. Many people live their lives without repentance. This is dangerous because we cannot fully experience the freedom of God without repentance. The Bible says that we are all sinners and have fallen short of the glory of God (Romans 3:23). Hence, we need to come to God and confess our sins to Him so He can heal us and give us an abundant life. Repentance is not a one-time action, but a lifestyle because we are all sinners and in need of redemption every day. Therefore, we need to live a life of repentance where we are sensitive to the voice of the Holy Spirit and are quick to repent when we are convicted for our sins.

The third step is forgiving those who have hurt us. This step is not always easy. Some people think they deserve to be hurt and do not deserve forgiveness. Unforgiveness is one of the bondages that may be unknown to us before we go to God for revelation. As I wrote this, the Holy Spirit emphasized that I should take time to explain how the devil steals our blessings when we do not forgive. Jesus stated that we should forgive always so we may be forgiven (Matthew 6:14-15).

Forgiveness is not an easy act. It requires the strength of God, especially when it is from people we once loved and trusted. As we call upon the name of God, He helps us forgive and forget as Jesus forgave His disciples who abandoned Him when He was crucified. Jesus knows how it feels to be betrayed and abandoned; He will help us forgive when we cannot do it ourselves.

After receiving the revelation of forgiveness, I had to forgive the people who hurt me in all seasons of my life and forgive myself before God could heal me. I started praying for all the people who hurt me, including my relatives. As I prayed for them, God reminded me that we are not fighting against flesh and blood. We are fighting against principalities not against people. The only enemy we have is the devil. This change in perspective was the beginning of my healing and my freedom from bondage. When I prayed for them, I would feel more peaceful and the anger and resentment toward them vanished. In Matthew 5:43-48, Jesus asked us to pray for those who oppress and persecute us. As we pray for those who broke our hearts, God starts to shift our perspective and starts to change us, before He changes the people who we are praying for. I realized that the more I prayed for the people who took my innocence, the more I would feel lighter and more at peace with myself and with God.

After we learn to forgive the people who have wronged us, we must forgive ourselves for all the things the enemy made us believe we were guilty of. In life, we sometimes give more credit to others than ourselves. In fact, it is easy to forgive someone else and not ourselves. We must come out of our victimization mindset so that God can free us and take us to a place of victory.

In my walk of healing, as I looked at the abuse that was done to me, I had to forgive myself for not fighting back the first time it happened. The devil made me believe I was responsible for how my relative abused me for three years. I was angry at myself for allowing him to take my innocence and destroy my youth. That was the hardest step to go through because I had to face all my failures, acknowledge that I was not responsible for what happened to me, and forgive myself. I poured out my pain to God and asked Him to give me a revelation about how He saw me. After the healing of self-hurt and forgiving others, I had to learn to build healthy relationships where I could guard my heart and learn to grow from my pain. I realized that pain was teaching me and stretching my faith and dependency on God after realizing that only God could give me the love my heart needs.

The road to forgiving myself was the hardest one because I had to forgive myself for the unwise decisions I made out of frustration. I was living to please people and to be validated by others, and I sometimes took the wrong road. By surrendering all my walks and paths of disobedience to God, the Holy Spirit finally gave me a chance to walk in truth with myself and forgive all the actions I took.

I had to rediscover myself and learn to love myself before I could love others. We need to take time to discover who we are beneath the surface and embrace ourselves before we can love others in a healthy way. We cannot give what we do not have. If we do not have the revelation of our identity, our relationships can suffer when we pretend to be what we are not and compromise ourselves because we fear being who we truly are. I came to realize these truths as I was writing this book. God continued to heal my heart and took me to deeper layers of my heart, which I never thought needed healing.

In your steps toward healing, you need to face yourself and discover who you truly are. This process can be hard because we tend to live differently than what we really feel, especially when our relationships take away from us instead of building us and growing us. This process may be scary at first. It requires digging deeper in our hearts and awakening any pain that may have been forgotten. God does not want you to remember your pain and be hurt, but He reminds you about the pain so He can take it forever. He heals you and gives you a platform to edify other people who may be facing what you have overcome. God heals us so we may be a living testimony for others.

I would like to end by emphasizing the power of your story. As you read this, you may be grateful to God for overcoming what I went through and forgetting what you have overcome in your life. My goal is that you take the step to healing and walk in freedom by sharing your story with others the way God will allow you to. This does not mean you will be asked to write a book or do what someone else did, but God will show you how to impact the people He brings in your life. I believe we have different purposes, and your purpose is found in what you have overcome. God created us uniquely so that we can walk in freedom and fulfill what He created us for.

Many of you may wonder what your purpose is or why God created you. The enemy always wants to make us think we are all the same and have no unique purpose. God created each one of us with a different path and purpose. As you invite God into your life and submit to Him, He will show you what your purpose is. He alone knows what He created you for, and as you walk in healing and freedom, He will open the door of your purpose for you to walk in.

I would like to invite you into a relationship that will change the trajectory of your life. When you receive Jesus into your life, He comes in and changes everything in you.

> *"Here I am! I stand at the door and knock. If anyone hears my voice and opens the door, I will come in and eat with that person, and they with me." (Revelation 3:20)*

Jesus is waiting at the door of your heart. He is waiting for you to open your heart so He may heal you and free you. My life changed when I opened my heart to Him and allowed Him to heal me and strengthen me, which led me to write this book.

If you feel like you've never had a relationship with Jesus and feel it is time to experience a true relationship with Him, there is no better time to do it than now. Jesus died for you and me so we can walk in perfect healing and transformation in Him.

The goal of this book is to bring the salvation of Jesus Christ to you because only He can take you from bondage to freedom. He will walk beside you and renew you for His glory. As you decide to welcome Jesus into your life, take some time to think about how loving He is toward you and how He wants to set you free. He wants you to live an abundant life in Him.

My prayer for you is that you find hope and joy as you read the next lines and feel refreshed in the presence of God. If He freed me from bondage, He can do the same for you. He can do even greater things in and through you when you avail yourself.

> *Now a slave has no permanent place in the family, but a son belongs to it forever. So, if the Son sets you free, you will be free indeed. (John 8:35-36)*

We are sons and daughters of God when we accept Jesus Christ as our Lord and Savior. Jesus is the only one who can change your story and turn your pain into purpose and your mess into a message of freedom. Jesus is the only way to freedom, and He is the redeemer of our souls. He knew you before you were born and set you apart for a great purpose:

> *"Before I formed you in the womb, I knew you, before you were born, I set you apart; I appointed you as a prophet to the nations." (Jeremiah 1:5)*

Just as Jeremiah was appointed a prophet in his mother's womb, God knew you in your mother's womb. He knew what you would be. Although the devil tried to destroy your life, God kept you this far so you can know there is a hope for your future. You can encounter the hope of the world: Jesus Christ.

Jesus died so you and I could have abundant life. Although life sometimes brings pain and disappointment, God is always here to show us that we can overcome them and live lives of freedom. We don't have to stay in pain. He can turn our pain into purpose and our tests into testimonies. You are a step away from healing and freedom.

If you need to experience God's freedom, you can welcome Jesus into your life as you pray this short prayer with all your heart. I believe that Jesus will come into your heart and give you a new start as you welcome Him in your heart. I pray that Jesus will encounter you and that His love will never cease in your heart as you walk a path of healing and freedom. Say this prayer:

Lord Jesus, I believe you are the Son of God, my Savior. Forgive me of all my sins; make me a new creation in You. Today, I give You my life, my heart, and give You everything of me. Come in and free me from all chains and hurt. Thank You for welcoming me into Your kingdom. I am a child of God.

As you prayed this prayer with all your heart, I believe Jesus came into your heart. From this moment, you are a new creation; your past is forgiven. Jesus will start to heal your heart in steps little by little. I encourage you to get a Bible and a journal to write all the revelations you will get as you start reading the Word of God. This will grow your faith, draw you closer to God, and guide you into the path God created for you to walk. The Word of God is the very breath of our Lord and His Word will direct you, teach you and give you the wisdom and knowledge you need to fulfill your purpose and live in freedom from bondage.

All scripture is God-breathed and is useful for teaching, correcting, and training in righteousness, so that the servant of God may be thoroughly equipped for every good work. (2 Timothy 3:16-17)

As you read the Word of God and meditate on it, the Holy Spirit will give you more revelations. In every season you walk through, He will give you weapons to fight the devil. Jesus did not fight the devil with any weapons besides the Word of God (Matthew 4:1-11). Therefore, you need to know what the Bible says about everything you face to fight the enemy from the source just as Jesus did.

After you get a Bible and journal to pray and meditate on the Word of God, you need to find a church where you can be planted and surround yourself with people of God who can grow your faith and share your pain when needed.

King David mentioned how the righteous children of God flourish when they are planted in the house of God (Psalm 92:12-13). It is important to worship God with others in a church. Although it is not mandatory to attend a church, I believe everyone needs to have leadership covering and fellowship with other Christians. Jesus said that wherever two or three people are gathered in His name, He is with them (Matthew 18:20). Hence, prayer has more power when it is done with other people who share your faith.

As you read the Word of God, meditate on the Word, and attend a church community, God will align you with people who will bless you and hold you in painful times: "As iron sharpens iron, so one person sharpens another." (Proverbs 27:17).

I pray that God will bless you and strengthen you as you walk from bondage to freedom and experience the abundant life of Christ.

To Jesus Christ be the honor and power forever and ever. Amen.

References

Haperen, M. V. (2012). The Holocaust and Other Genocides: An Introduction. Amsterdam: NIOD Institute for War.